GOLDEN MORNING

2015 SPRING COLLECTION
by Knit Picks

Printed in the United States of America

First Printing, 2015

ISBN 978-1-62767-073-9

Versa Press, Inc
800-447-7829

www.versapress.com

CONTENTS

Introduction

A golden morning means a new day is dawning, brimming with promise, ready for anything, unspoiled and perfect. It's the best time to enjoy a moment of quiet meditation, optimistic expectation and handmade whimsy. Our 2015 Spring Collection, *Golden Morning*, is inspired by that glorious time of day when things are just beginning to stir in the early light. The fifteen garments inside will give you lightweight projects you'll love to knit. From striped pullovers like Nautical, to the Elva, a lacy cardigan, to tops with striking details like the Kayden Tank, you'll find a project sure to become your essential garment for warm weather. These breezy pieces are easy to wear on their own or layered, with enough style to take you from sunrise to sunset and beyond. So brew some tea and settle into the peace and ease of a *Golden Morning*.

ASTONISH TOP

by Katy Banks

FINISHED MEASUREMENTS

32 (36, 40, 44, 48, 52, 56, 60, 64)" finished bust measurement; garment is meant to be worn with 2" of positive ease

YARN

Knit Picks Lindy Chain (70% Linen, 30% Pima Cotton; 180 yards/50g):
MC Swan 26447, 3 (4, 4, 5, 5, 6, 7, 7, 8) balls
CC Honey 26458, 1 (1, 1, 2, 2, 2, 2, 2, 2) balls

NEEDLES

US 2 (3mm) 24" or longer circular depending on size knit, or size to obtain gauge

US 2 (3mm) DPNs or two 24" circular needles for two circulars technique, or one 32" or longer circular needle for Magic Loop technique, or size to obtain gauge

NOTIONS

Yarn Needle
Stitch Marker

GAUGE

30 sts and 38 rows = 4" in St st, blocked

Astonish Top

Notes:

This top is knit in two pieces worked on the bias; each beginning with one stitch in the bottom corner. After the front and back pieces are completed, blocked, and seamed, short bands are picked up and worked around each opening to finish the piece.

Cable Cast-On (worked flat)

Insert the right needle between the first and second sts on the left needle, draw up a loop, place the loop on the left needle. One st CO. Repeat until desired number of sts are CO.

Seed Stitch (worked in the round over an odd number of sts)

Rnd 1: K1, *P1, K1, repeat from * to the end of the round.
Rnd 2: P1, *K1, P1, repeat from * to the end of the round.
Repeat Rnds 1 and 2 for pat.

DIRECTIONS

As you work from section to section in a piece of the garment, you will always continue with the row number where you left off. For example, if you end one section with Row 8, you should begin the next section with Row 9.

Whenever you are working the yo from a previous row, work it through the back loop so the yo st is twisted. This provides a non-directional increase which causes the least amount of stitch distortion.

Back Piece

Create a slip knot with MC and place on the needle.
Preparation Row 1 (RS): Kfb (2 sts on needle)
Preparation Row 2 (WS): Pfb, Pfb (4 sts on needle)
Continue with Row 3 below.

Increase Both Edges Section

Row 1 (RS): Change to MC, K1, yo, K to the end. 1 st inc.
Rows 2, 4, 10, 12 (WS): P1, yo, P to the last st, yo, P1. 2 sts inc.
Rows 3, 5, 9, 11: K1, yo, K to the last st, yo, K1. 2 sts inc.
Row 6: P1, yo, P to the end. 1 st inc.
Row 7: Knit.
Row 8: P to the last st, yo, P1. 1 st inc.
Row 13: Change to CC, K to the last st, yo, K1. 1 st inc.
Row 14: Knit.
Continue this 14-row repeat until the right edge of your triangle (i.e., the bottom of the Back piece) measures 16 (18, 20, 22, 24, 26, 28, 30, 32)".

Increase Left Edge, Decrease Right Edge Section

Row 1: Change to MC, K1, ssk, K to the end. 1 st dec.
Rows 2, 4, 10, 12: P1, yo, P to the last 3 sts, P2tog-tbl, P1.
Rows 3, 5, 9, 11: K1, ssk, K to the last st, yo, K1.
Row 6: P1, yo, P to the end. 1 st inc.
Row 7: Knit.
Row 8: P to the last 3 sts, P2tog-tbl, P1. 1 st dec.
Row 13: Change to CC, K to the last st, yo, K1. 1 st inc.
Row 14: Knit.
Continue this 14-row repeat until the left edge (i.e., the left side of the Back piece) measures 20 (21.5, 22.5, 24.5, 25.25, 26.25, 27.25, 28.25, 29.25)".

Decrease Both Edges Section

Row 1 (RS): Change to MC, K1, ssk, K to the end. 1 st dec.
Rows 2, 4, 10, 12 (WS): P1, P2tog, P to the last 3 sts, P2tog-tbl, P1. 2 sts dec.
Rows 3, 5, 9, 11: K1, ssk, K to the last 3 sts, K2tog, K1. 2 sts dec.
Row 6: P1, P2tog, P to the end. 1 st dec.
Row 7: Knit.
Row 8: P to the last 3 sts, P2tog-tbl, P1. 1 st dec.
Row 13: Change to CC, K to the last 3 sts, K2tog, K1. 1 st dec.
Row 14: Knit.
Continue this 14-row repeat until you have only 1 st remaining. Break the yarn and pull it through the last st to secure it.

Front Piece

Begin as for the Back Piece, working the 2 Preparation Rows and then work the Increase Both Edges Section until the left edge of your triangle (i.e., the right side of the Front piece) measures 13.5 (14.5, 15, 16.5, 16.75, 17.25, 17.75, 18.25, 18.75)", ending with a WS row.

Left Edge Even, Increase Right Edge Section

Working from the left edge and using the Cable CO Method, CO 49 (53, 56, 60, 64, 68, 71, 75, 79) sts.
Row 1 (RS): Change to MC, K1, yo, K to the end. 1 st inc.
Rows 2, 4, 8, 10, 12 (WS): P to the last st, yo, P1. 1 st inc.
Rows 3, 5, 9, 11: K1, yo, K to the end. 1 st inc.
Row 6: Purl.
Row 7: Knit.
Row 13: Change to CC, K to end.
Row 14: Knit.
Continue this 14-row repeat until right edge (i.e., the bottom of the Front piece) measures 16 (18, 20, 22, 24, 26, 28, 30, 32)".

Left Edge Even, Decrease Right Edge Section

Row 1: Change to MC, K1, ssk, K to the end. 1 st dec.
Rows 2, 4, 8, 10, 12: P to the last 3 sts, P2tog-tbl, P1. 1 st dec.
Rows 3, 5, 9, 11: K1, ssk, K to the end. 1 st dec.
Row 6: Purl.
Row 7: Knit.
Row 13: Change to CC, K to end.
Row 14: Knit.
Continue this 14-row repeat until the left edge measures 5 (5.75, 6.75, 7.5, 8, 8.75, 9.5, 10.25, 11)" from the last CO row.

Decrease Both Edges Section

Work as for the Decrease Both Edges Section for the Back.
Continue until the right edge (i.e., the left side of the Front piece) measures 13.5 (14.5, 15, 16.5, 16.75, 17.25, 17.75, 18.25, 18.75)".

Decrease Left Edge, Right Edge Even Section

Row 1: Change to MC, K to end.
Row 2, 4, 6, 10, 12: P1, P2tog, P to the end. 1 st dec.
Row 3, 5, 9, 11: K to the last 3 sts, K2tog, K1. 1 st dec.
Row 7: Knit.
Row 8: Purl.
Row 13: Change to CC, K to the last 3 sts, K2tog, K1. 1 st dec.
Row 14: Knit.
Continue this 14-row repeat until the right edge measures 6.5 (7, 7.5, 8, 8.5, 9, 9.5, 10, 10.5)" from the point where you began working that edge even.

Finishing

Weave in ends. Wash and block to diagrams. Seam pieces along each 13.5 (14.5, 15, 16.5, 16.75, 17.25, 17.75, 18.25, 18.75)" side seam and along each 5 (5.75, 6.75, 7.5, 8, 8.75, 9.5, 10.25, 11)" shoulder seam.

Hem and Cuffs

With MC and circular needle, PU and K 239 (269, 299, 329, 359, 389, 419, 449, 479) sts around bottom of garment. Place marker for beginning of round. Work in Seed Stitch until hem band is about 1.5" or desired length. BO sts in pat.

Using DPNs or 2-circulars or Magic Loop method, with MC, PU and K 97 (105, 113, 119, 127, 135, 143, 149, 157) sts around one arm opening. Place marker for beginning of round. Work in Seed Stitch until cuff is about 1.5" or desired length. BO sts in pat. Repeat for the other cuff.

Drape Neck Facing

With MC and RS facing, pick up and K about 3 sts for every 4 rows along the neck opening. Place marker for beginning of round. P 1 rnd, K 4 rnds and BO.

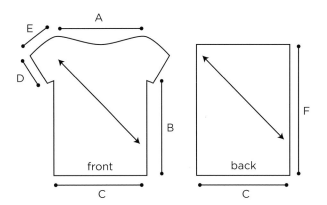

A 19 (20.5, 21.5, 22.5, 25, 26.5, 28, 29.5, 31)"
B 13.5 (14.5, 15, 16.5, 16.75, 17.25, 17.75, 18.25, 18.75)"
C 16 (18, 20, 22, 24, 26, 28, 30, 32)"
D 6.5 (7, 7.5, 8, 8.5, 9, 9.5, 10, 10.5)"
E 5 (5.75, 6.75, 7.75, 8, 8.75, 9.5, 10.25, 11)"
F 20 (21.5, 22.5, 24.5, 25.5, 26.25, 27.25, 28.25, 29.25)"

BRANDILYN TOP

by Quenna Lee

FINISHED MEASUREMENTS

38.5 (40.75, 43, 45.75, 48.75, 52.25, 56.75, 60.25, 64.75)″ finished bust measurement; garment is meant to be worn with 6-7″ of positive ease.

YARN

Knit Picks Lindy Chain (70% Linen, 30% Pima Cotton; 180 yards/50g): Silver 26453, 5 (5, 5, 6, 6, 6, 7, 7, 8) balls

NEEDLES

US 5 (3.75mm) 24″ or longer circular needle depending on garment size, plus DPNs or needles for small circumference knitting, or size to obtain gauge.

NOTIONS

Cable Needle
Scrap Yarn or Stitch Holders
Spare DPNs
Stitch Markers
Yarn Needle

GAUGE

22 sts and 30 rows = 4″ over Stockinette St in the round, blocked.
22 sts and 32 rows = 4″ over Stockinette St in the round, unblocked.

Brandilyn Top

Notes:

This easy top is worked in one piece from the bottom up. At the underarm, the body is divided into front and back and worked back and forth. The sleeves are picked up from the armhole and worked from the top down.

Since the recommended yarn relaxes after blocking, the unblocked row gauge is used to determine vertical measurements in the pattern. If the row gauge remains constant after blocking, use the blocked measurements in the schematic.

If you're unable to achieve the unblocked row gauge, determine the vertical measurements using the following calculation: Unblocked vertical measurement = (blocked/final measurement multiplied by blocked row gauge per inch) divided by unblocked row gauge per inch.

Garter Stitch (worked flat over any number of sts)
All Rows: Knit all sts.

Garter Stitch (in the rnd over any number of sts)
Rnd 1: Knit all sts.
Rnd 2: Purl all sts.
Rep Rnds 1-2 for pat.

Stockinette Stitch (St st, worked flat or in the round over any number of sts)
Worked Flat: Knit on RS rows, P on WS rows.
Worked In the Round: Knit all sts of every row.

Right Mock Pleat
Sl 3 sts onto CN, place CN in back, *k2tog the next st on left needle and 1st from CN, rep from * twice.

Left Mock Pleat
Sl 3 sts knitwise onto CN, place CN in front, *ssk the 1st from CN and the next st on left needle, rep from * twice.

Wrap & Turn (W&T)
Work until the stitch to be wrapped. If knitting: Bring yarn to the front of the work, slip next st as if to purl, return the yarn to the back; turn work and slip wrapped st onto RH needle. Continue across row. If purling: Bring yarn to the back of the work, slip next st as if to purl, return the yarn to the front; turn work and slip wrapped st onto RH needle. Continue across row.
Picking up wraps: Work to the wrapped st. If knitting, insert the RH needle under the wrap(s), then through the wrapped st kwise. Knit the wrap(s) together with the wrapped st. If purling, slip the wrapped st pwise onto the RH needle, and use the LH needle to lift the wrap(s) and place them on the RH needle. Slip wrap(s) and unworked st back to LH needle; purl all together through the back loop.

3-Needle BO
* Hold the two pieces of knitting together with the points facing to the right. Insert a third needle into the first st on each of the needles Kwise, starting with the front needle. Work a knit st, pulling the loop through both of the sts you've inserted the third needle through. After pulling the loop through, sl the first st off of each of the needles.

Repeat from *. Pass the first finished st over the second and off of the needle.

Neck I-cord BO (RS)
CO 2 sts and return both sts to left needle. *K1, ssk, return 2 sts to left needle, rep from * to last 2 sts, BO. Pull yarn through final st to fasten off. Seam ends together.

DIRECTIONS
Body
Hem
CO 112 (118, 124, 132, 140, 150, 162, 172, 184) sts, PM, CO 112 (118, 124, 132, 140, 150, 162, 172, 184) sts, PM for beginning of rnd and join to begin working in the rnd, being careful not to twist sts. 224 (236, 248, 264, 280, 300, 324, 344, 368) sts. Work Garter Stitch for 8 rnds.

A-line Shaping
Dec Rnd: K6, k2tog, K to 8 sts before next marker, ssk, K6, SM, K6, k2tog, K to 8 sts before next marker, ssk, K6. 4 sts dec.
Rep Dec Rnd every 46th rnd 2 more times. 212 (224, 236, 252, 268, 288, 312, 332, 356) sts. Work in St st until piece measures 14.5 (14.5, 14.5, 14.5, 14, 14, 14, 14, 14)" unblocked.
Next Rnd: K30 (33, 36, 40, 44, 49, 55, 60, 66), PM, K46, PM, K30 (33, 36, 40, 44, 49, 55, 60, 66), SM, K32 (35, 38, 41, 45, 50, 56, 60, 66), PM, K42 (42, 42, 44, 44, 44, 44, 46, 46), PM, K32 (35, 38, 41, 45, 50, 56, 60, 66) to end of rnd.

Divide for Front and Back
Divide for armholes: Place last 106 (112, 118, 126, 134, 144, 156, 166, 178) sts worked on a holder for front. 106 (112, 118, 126, 134, 144, 156, 166, 178) sts on needle for back.

Back
Note: Mock Pleat Row begins before Armhole shaping is completed. Please read ahead before proceeding.

Armhole Shaping
BO 3 (4, 4, 6, 6, 7, 9, 9, 10) sts at beginning of next 2 rows. BO 2 (2, 2, 3, 3, 3, 5, 4, 5) sts at the beginning of next 2 (2, 2, 2, 2, 2, 4, 4) rows. 10 (12, 12, 18, 18, 20, 28, 34, 40) sts dec. 96 (100, 106, 108, 116, 124, 128, 132, 138) sts.

On the next RS row, begin Mock Pleat Row: K2, k2tog, K to marker, remove marker, *Right Mock Pleat, K2, rep from * 3 times total, *Left Mock Pleat, K2, rep from * 2 times total, Left Mock Pleat, remove marker, K last 4 sts, ssk, K2. 20 sts dec.

Purl 1 row. 76 (80, 86, 88, 96, 104, 108, 112, 118) sts.

Dec Row (RS): K2, k2tog, K to last 4 sts, ssk, K2. 2 sts dec.
Rep Dec Row every RS row 4 (5, 6, 7, 9, 11, 11, 10, 10) more times. 66 (68, 72, 72, 76, 80, 84, 90, 96) sts.
Work in St st until armhole measures 6 (6.25, 6.5, 6.75, 7.25, 7.5, 8, 8.5, 9)" unblocked, ending after a WS row.

Neck Shaping
On the RS, while continuing in St st, K18 (18, 20, 20, 22, 22, 24, 24, 26) right shoulder sts and place on holder. Drop yarn. Join second ball of yarn and BO 30 (32, 32, 32, 32, 36, 36, 42, 44) sts, K18 (18, 20, 20, 22, 22, 24, 24, 26) left shoulder sts to the end.
Work one WS row.

Left Shoulder Shaping

Shoulder Neck Shaping (RS): K2, ssk, K to end. 1 st dec.
Purl 1 row.

Rep last 2 rows 1 more time. 16 (16, 18, 18, 20, 20, 22, 22, 24) sts.
Work in St st until armhole measures 6.5 (6.75, 7, 7.25, 7.75, 8, 8.5, 9, 9.5)" unblocked, ending after a WS row.

Short Row 1 (RS): K10 (10, 12, 12, 13, 13, 14, 14, 16) sts, W&T.
Purl to end.

Short Row 2 (RS): K5 (5, 6, 6, 6, 6, 7, 7, 8) sts, W&T.
Purl to end.

Next Row (RS): Knit all sts, knitting wraps together with wrapped sts.
Work in pat for 3 rows. Break yarn, leaving a 20" tail. Place sts on holder.

Right Shoulder Shaping

Transfer right shoulder sts to needle, ready to work a WS row.
Purl 1 row.

Shoulder Neck Shaping (RS): K to last 4 sts, k2tog, K2.
Purl 1 row.
Rep last 2 rows 1 more time. 16 (16, 18, 18, 20, 20, 22, 22, 24) sts.
Work in St st until armhole measures 6.5 (6.75, 7, 7.25, 7.75, 8, 8.5, 9, 9.5)" unblocked, ending after a RS row.

Short Row 1 (WS): P10 (10, 12, 12, 13, 13, 14, 14, 16) sts, W&T.
Knit to end.

Short Row 2 (WS): P5 (5, 6, 6, 6, 6, 7, 7, 8) sts, W&T.
Knit to end.

Next Row (WS): Purl all sts, purling wraps together with wrapped sts.
Work in pat for 2 rows. Break yarn, leaving a 20" tail. Place sts on holder.

Front

Note: Mock Pleat Row and Garter Bodice may begin before Armhole shaping is completed. Please read ahead before proceeding.

Armhole Shaping

Transfer 106 (112, 118, 126, 134, 144, 156, 166, 178) sts to needle. BO 3 (4, 4, 6, 6, 7, 9, 9, 10) sts at beginning of next 2 rows. BO 2 (2, 2, 3, 3, 3, 5, 4, 5) sts at the beginning of next 2 (2, 2, 2, 2, 2, 4, 4) rows. 10 (12, 12, 18, 18, 20, 28, 34, 40) sts dec. 96 (100, 106, 108, 116, 124, 128, 132, 138) sts.

On the next RS row, begin Mock Pleat Row: K2, k2tog, K to marker, SM, *Right Mock Pleat, K1, rep from * once, Right Mock Pleat, K2 (2, 2, 4, 4, 4, 4, 6, 6), *Left Mock Pleat, K1, rep from * once, Left Mock Pleat, SM, K last 4 sts, ssk, K2. 20 sts dec. 20 sts dec. Purl 1 row. 76 (80, 86, 88, 96, 104, 108, 112, 118) sts rem.

Begin Garter Bodice **AT THE SAME TIME** as the Dec Rows.

Dec Row (RS): K2, k2tog, K to last 4 sts, ssk, K2. 2 sts dec.
Rep Dec Row each RS row 4 (5, 6, 7, 9, 11, 11, 10, 10) more times. 66 (68, 72, 72, 76, 80, 84, 90, 96) sts after armhole shaping and Right and Left Mock Pleats are completed.

Garter Bodice Row (RS): Work to 5 (6, 6, 5, 5, 7, 7, 9, 10) sts before marker, PM, K5 (6, 6, 5, 5, 7, 7, 9, 10) sts, remove marker, K24 (24, 24, 26, 26, 26, 26, 28, 28), remove marker, K5 (6, 6, 5, 5, 7, 7, 9, 10) sts, PM, work to end of row.

Next Row (WS): Purl to marker, SM, K34 (36, 36, 36, 36, 40, 40, 46, 48), SM, purl to end. Rep last 2 rows until armhole measures 2.75 (3, 3.25, 3, 3.5, 3.75, 3.75, 4.25, 4.75)" unblocked, ending after a WS row.

Neck Shaping

On the RS, while continuing in St st, K16 (16, 18, 18, 20, 20, 22, 22, 24) left shoulder sts and place on holder. Drop yarn. Join second ball of yarn and BO 34 (36, 36, 36, 36, 40, 40, 46, 48) sts, K16 (16, 18, 18, 20, 20, 22, 22, 24) right shoulder sts to the end.
Work in St st until armhole measures 6.5 (6.75, 7, 7.25, 7.75, 8, 8.5, 9, 9.5)" unblocked, ending after a WS row.

Right Shoulder Shaping

Short Row 1 (RS): K10 (10, 12, 12, 13, 13, 14, 14, 16) sts, W&T.
Purl to end.
Short Row 2 (RS): K5 (5, 6, 6, 6, 6, 7, 7, 8) sts, W&T.
Purl to end.
Next Row (RS): K all sts, knitting wraps together with wrapped sts.

Work in pat for 3 rows. Break yarn, leaving a 20" tail. Place sts on holder.

Left Shoulder Shaping

Transfer left shoulder sts to needle, ready to work a WS row.
Work in St st until armhole measures 6.5 (6.75, 7, 7.25, 7.75, 8, 8.5, 9, 9.5)" unblocked, ending after a RS row.

Short Row 1 (WS): P10 (10, 12, 12, 13, 13, 14, 14, 16) sts, W&T.
Knit to end.
Short Row 2 (WS): P5 (5, 6, 6, 6, 6, 7, 7, 8) sts, W&T.
Knit to end.
Next Row (WS): Purl all sts, purling wraps together with wrapped sts.

Work in pat for 2 rows. Break yarn, leaving a 20" tail. Place sts on holder.

Sleeves (make 2)

Note: Sleeve cap is worked back and forth before joining together to work in the rnd.

With RS facing, seam shoulders using 3-Needle BO.
On the RS, starting at the center of underarm, evenly PU and K72 (76, 80, 82, 86, 94, 104, 112, 118) sts.

Set Up Row: P12 (12, 13, 13, 14, 15, 17, 18, 19), PM, P15 (17, 17, 18, 18, 21, 22, 24, 26), PM, P18 (18, 20, 20, 22, 22, 26, 28, 28), PM, P15 (17, 17, 18, 18, 21, 22, 24, 26), PM, P12 (12, 13, 13, 14, 15, 17, 18, 19).

Shape sleeve cap with short rows worked in Garter st:
Row 1 (RS): K to third marker, remove marker, W&T.
Row 2 (WS): K to second marker, remove marker, W&T.
Rows 3–6 K to wrapped st, work wrap together with wrapped st, K1, W&T.
Rows 7–8: K to wrapped st, work wrap together with wrapped st, W&T.

Rep Rows 7-8 an additional 9 (11, 11, 12, 12, 15, 16, 18, 20) times until first and fourth marker are reached. On the last RS row, K to end of row and PM for beg of rnd, knitting wrap(s) together with wrapped st(s) as you come to them, removing first and fourth marker.

Begin to work in rnd, switching to DPNs if necessary. Continue in Garter Stitch (in the rnd) until sleeve measures 2.75 (2.75, 2.75, 3.25, 3.25, 3.25, 3.75, 3.75, 3.75)" unblocked, from underarm. BO in pat.

Neck Edging

With RS facing up and starting at the right corner of the back neck BO, PU and K30 (32, 32, 32, 32, 36, 36, 42, 44) sts from back neck BO, PU and K30 (30, 30, 32, 32, 32, 35, 35, 35) along left side, PU and K34 (36, 36, 36, 36, 40, 40, 46, 48) sts from front neck BO, and PU and K30 (30, 30, 32, 32, 32, 35, 35, 35) along right side. 124 (128, 128, 132, 132, 140, 146, 158, 162) sts. BO with Neck I-cord BO.

Finishing

Weave in ends and block to measurements.

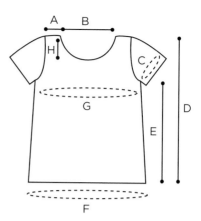

A 3 (3, 3.25, 3.25, 3.75, 3.75, 4, 4, 4.25)"
B 6.25 (6.5, 6.5, 6.5, 6.5, 7.25, 7.25, 8.25, 8.75)"
C 13 (13.75, 14.5, 15, 15.75, 17, 19, 20.25, 21.5)"
D 23.5 (23.75, 24, 24.25, 24.25, 24.5, 25, 25.5 26)"
E 15.5 (15.5, 15.5, 15.5, 15, 15, 15, 15, 15)"
F 40.75 (43, 45, 48, 51, 54.5, 59, 62.5, 67)"
G 38.5 (40.75, 43, 45.75, 48.75, 52.25, 56.75, 60.25, 64.75)"
H 4 (4, 4, 4.5, 4.5, 4.5, 5, 5, 5)"

BUDDINA VEST

by Amber Bertram

FINISHED MEASUREMENTS

27 (30.25, 34, 37.75, 41.25, 45.25, 49, 53, 56.75)" finished bust measurement; garment is meant to be worn with approx 2" of negative ease

YARN

Knit Picks Comfy Fingering (75% Pima Cotton, 25% Acrylic; 218 yards/50g): MC Semolina 24819, 2 (2, 2, 2, 2, 2, 2, 3, 3) balls, CC White 24812, 1 (1, 1, 2, 2, 2, 2, 2, 2) balls

NEEDLES

US 7 (4.50mm) 2 sets of 24" or longer circular needles, or size to obtain gauge

NOTIONS

Yarn Needle
Stitch Markers (optional)
Smooth Waste Yarn (for provisional cast on)
Stitch Holders

GAUGE

24 sts and 30 rows = 4" over lace pattern, blocked

Buddina Vest

Notes:

This simple shrug cardigan is worked from the bottom up. Beginning with a provisional cast on to create a tidy folded hem, it's worked in one piece to the underarms where the fronts and back are split and worked separately. A three-needle bind off is used to join the shoulders, and the front band is picked up and worked last.

Stitch Pattern (worked flat)

Row 1 (RS): K2 (6, 5, 4, 3, 3, 2, 2, 7), *yo, ssk, K10, repeat from * to last 4 (8, 7, 6, 5, 5, 4, 4, 9) sts, yo, ssk, K to end.

Row 2 (WS): Purl.

Row 3 (RS): K2 (6, 5, 4, 3, 3, 2, 2, 7), *K2tog, yo, K10, repeat from * to last 4 (8, 7, 6, 5, 5, 4, 4, 9) sts, K2tog, yo, K to end

Row 4 (WS): Purl.

Repeat Rows 1-4 for stitch pattern.

Provisional Cast On (PCO):

Using waste yarn, cast on as normal. Knit two or three rows, then knit one row in working yarn and carry on with instructions as directed. Note: This is the simplest way to work a PCO, any alternative PCO can be used if desired.

3-Needle Bind Off

With the two pieces of knitting on separate needles, hold together with right sides facing. Using a third needle, purl the first stitch of the rear needle together with the first stitch of the front needle. Purl the second stitches of each needle together in the same manner. Lift the first purled stitch over the second purled stitch on the right hand needle as if binding off normally (one stitch bound off). Purl the next stitch on each needle together as before and lift the first stitch on the right needle over the second as before (two stitches bound off). Continue binding off stitches in this way until all stitches are bound off.

DIRECTIONS

Using MC and waste yarn, PCO 150 (170, 192, 214, 236, 260, 282, 306, 328) sts.

Hem

Row 1 (WS): Purl.

Row 2 (RS): Knit.

Rows 3-4: Repeat Rows 1-2.

Row 5 (WS): Knit.

Row 6 (RS): Knit.

Row 7: Purl.

Rows 8-9: Repeat Rows 6-7.

Remove the waste yarn from PCO, placing live stitches on a spare needle. With the RS facing, fold the work so the PCO row is held behind, and knit both rows together as follows:

Row 10: K2tog (one st from the working row and one st from the PCO row) to end.

Purl 1 WS row.

Body

Beginning with Row 1, work two repeats of stitch pattern, then change to CC. Working in a stripe pattern of 12 rows (3 pattern repeats) of CC and 12 rows (3 pattern repeats) of MC, continue until work measures 6.5 (6.25, 6, 5.75, 5.5, 5, 5, 4.5, 4.5)" from folded edge, ending with a WS row.

Right Front

Maintaining stitch pattern and stripes as established, work across 25 (29, 34, 39, 44, 50, 55, 61, 66) sts, K2, turn. Continue working Right Front on these 27 (31, 36, 41, 46, 52, 57, 63, 68) sts only.

Row 1 (WS): Sl2, P to end.

Row 2 (RS): Work in pattern to last 2 sts, K2.

From here on, the 2 sts at the armhole edge will be worked as K2 (RS) and Sl2 (WS) for a neat selvage. Continue working in pattern as established until Right Front piece measures 15.5 (15.75, 16, 16.25, 16.5, 16.5, 17, 17, 17.5)" from folded edge, ending with a RS row. Break yarn and leave sts on a stitch holder.

Left Front

Slip the next 96 (108, 120, 132, 144, 156, 168, 180, 192) sts onto a stitch holder to work the Back later. Rejoin yarn, ready to work a RS row. Continue working Left Front on the remaining 27 (31, 36, 41, 46, 52, 57, 63, 68) sts only.

Row 1 (RS): Sl2, work in pattern to end.

Row 2 (WS): P to end.

From here on, the 2 sts at the armhole edge will be worked as Sl2 (RS) and P2 (WS) for a neat selvage. Continue working in pattern as established until Left Front piece measures same as Right Front, ending with a RS row. Break yarn and leave stitches on a stitch holder.

Back

Replace Back stitches onto working needle. Rejoin yarn, ready to work a RS row.

Row 1 (RS): Sl2, work in pattern to last 2 sts, K2.

Row 2 (WS): Sl2, P to end.

From here on, the 2 sts at each armhole edge will be worked as Sl2 and K2 (RS) and Sl2 and P2 (WS) for a neat selvage. Continue working in pattern as established until Back measures the same as the Front pieces, ending with a RS row.

Do not break yarn.

Place the live stitches from the right front on a spare needle and, holding behind the working needle (with RS facing), join the shoulders by working a three-needle bind off until all Right Front stitches are incorporated.

Using a standard bind off, continue across the back neck to bind off next 42 (46, 48, 50, 52, 52, 54, 54, 56) sts. Note: The last neck stitch bound off should be passed over the first K2tog of the three-needle bind off.

Place the live stitches from the Left Front on a spare needle and join the shoulders as before with a three-needle bind-off to end.

Front Band

Using MC and with RS facing, starting at the bottom of the Right Front, pick up 2 sts for every 3 rows up to Back neck bind off, pick up 1 st in each bound off st across Back neck, pick up 2 sts for every 3 rows down the Left Front to end. An exact stitch count is not necessary for this section.

Row 1 (WS): Sl2, P to end.

Row 2 (RS): Sl2, K to end.

Repeat these two rows until front band measures 2", ending with a purl row.

Bind off all sts loosely.

Finishing

Weave in ends, wash and block to diagram, leaving front band edge to roll naturally.

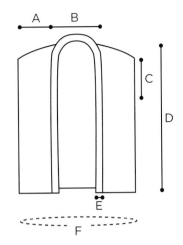

A 4.5 (5.25, 6, 6.75, 7.5, 8.5, 9.5, 10.5, 11.25)"
B 7 (7.5, 8, 8.25, 8.75, 8.75, 9, 9, 9.25)"
C 9 (9.5, 10, 10.5, 11, 11.5, 12, 12.5, 13)"
D 15.5 (15.75, 16, 16.25, 16.5, 16.5, 17, 17, 17.5)"
E 2" (not blocked)
F 25 (28.25, 32, 35.5, 39.25, 43.25, 47, 51, 54.5)"

CAROLYN'S CARDIGAN

by Geoffrey Hunnicutt

FINISHED MEASUREMENTS

36 (40, 44, 48, 52)" finished bust measurement; garment is meant to be worn with 3-4" of positive ease

YARN

Knit Picks Stroll Sock Yarn (75% Superwash Merino Wool, 25% Nylon; 231 yards/50g): Eggplant 25606, 6 (6, 7, 8, 8) balls

NEEDLES

US 6 (4mm) 24" or longer circular needles, or size to obtain gauge
US 4 (3.5mm) DPNs, or 2 sizes smaller than gauge needle

NOTIONS

Stitch Markers
Scrap Yarn or Stitch Holder
Size F or G Crochet Hook
Yarn Needle

GAUGE

24 sts and 26 rows = 4" over lace pattern on larger needles, blocked

Carolyn's Cardigan

Notes:

This lacy cardigan is knit in pieces sideways, beginning with the back which is knit in one piece from cuff to cuff. The left front is knit from the cuff to the body and the right front is knit from the body to the cuff.

The patterns are charted. The even (WS) rows have been omitted from the chart. All even (WS) rows are purled. When you encounter a double yarn over on a WS row, purl into the first yarn over and knit into the second.

Slip both the first and last stitches of each WS row purlwise.

Due to the elastic nature of the yarn and the lace pattern, wet blocking can be insufficient to maintain the blocked size. Running a hot steam iron over the blocked pieces before unpinning them will hold the size and shape. If you do not wish to do this step, you may lose up to an inch and a half as the material rebounds.

DIRECTIONS
Back

Using larger needles, CO 60 sts and begin Row 1 of Chart A. Knit in pattern through Row 117.
When you have finished Row 117, turn your work and CO 47 new sts using a knitted cast on. 163 sts.

Row 118 (WS): Purl back across your new CO sts and the other 116 sts.

Row 119: Work pattern as set across the new cast on sts until the last 7 sts. K4, P3.

Row 120: Purl.

Begin Charts B and C

Note that Chart B does not show the entire pattern. Rather, it shows the beginning and end portions. The first section shows the lace repeat that is knit across the work. The last section shows the end motif for the last 7 stitches.

Note: Chart C does not show the entire pattern. Rather, it shows the beginning and end portions. The first section shows the lace repeat that is knit across the work. The last section shows the pattern up to where the decreases happen.

Size 36": Begin Row 121. Continue until row 236 of Chart C. Omit the decreases and knit to end of Chart, binding off sts on Row 236 as noted below.

Size 40": Begin Row 121. Continue until row 248 of Chart C. Omit the decreases and knit to the end of Chart, binding off sts on Row 248 as noted below.

Size 44": Begin Row 121. Continue until row 260 of Chart C. Omit the decreases and knit to end of Chart, binding off sts on Row 260 as noted below .

Size 48": Begin Row 121. Continue until row 272 of Chart C. Omit the decreases and knit to end of Chart, binding off sts on Row 272 as noted below.

Size 52": Begin Row 121. Continue until row 284 of Chart C. Omit the decreases and knit to end of Chart, binding off sts on Row 284 as noted below.

Row 236 (248, 260, 272, 284) (WS): BO the first 47 stitches. Purl to end, slipping the last stitch purlwise.

Sleeve Decreases

All sizes will begin the sleeve decrease on Row 223 of Chart C. The lace pattern will jog a bit but it does not distract from the overall pattern.

Row 342: Bind off remaining 60 sts.

Left Front

The left front is worked the same as the back. To begin, with larger needles cast on 60 sts and begin Row 1 of Chart A. Continue working Charts A and B until Row 160 (166, 172, 178, 184). Bind off.

Right Front

The right front is worked the same as the back, starting from the long end and working out toward the cuff. Cast on 163 sts on larger needles. Following the same directions for back for Chart B through Chart C, Sleeve Decreases, but beginning right front at row 192 (185, 178, 171, 164).

Row 342: Bind Off.

Blocking

Before adding the front bands or the cuffs, the sweater must be blocked and seamed together.

Wash and block just the back to the size indicated. When the back piece has dried, and while it is still pinned in place, run a hot steam iron over the piece. This will help set the blocking.

Leave the back piece pinned down. Next, place the washed two front pieces over the back piece and pin to the size indicated. Pinning the front pieces to the back during blocking ensures the sleeve shape remains consistent between all three pieces.

When the front pieces have dried, run a hot steam iron over them. Seam the front to the back pieces together along the top of the sleeves and along the sides.

Front Band

Cast on 51 stitches onto larger needles. You will be knitting a K1, P1 rib. You want the band to be 6" wide. You may add or subtract stitches to get the correct width as long as you have an odd number of stitches.

Row 1: *K1, P1, rep from * until last st, K1.
Row 2: Slip 1 purlwise. *K1, P1, rep from * until last st. Slip last st purlwise.

Repeat Rows 1 and 2 until the piece measures 79". Place stitches on a holder.

Choose the best edge of the front band to be shown and then, starting with the bottom, sew the other edge to the inside left front bottom of the sweater. Continue to sew the front band up around the inside of the left front, across the back and down the right front.

Cuff (make 2)

Beginning at the bottom of the left sleeve, with smaller needles, PU and K 68 sts evenly around sleeve. Place a marker and join to work in the round.

Rnds 1-3: *K1, P1, rep from * to end of rnd.

Rnd 4: P2tog. Continue in 1x1 rib until last two sts, K2tog. 66 sts.

Rnds 5-7: Repeat Rnds 1-3.

Rnd 8: K2tog, P1. Continue in 1x1 rib until last two sts, P2tog. 64 sts.

Rnds 9-11: Repeat Rows 1-3

Rnd 12: P2tog. Continue in 1x1 rib until last two sts, K2tog. 62 sts.

Rnds 13-15: Repeat Rows 1-3

Rnd 16: K2tog, P1. Continue in 1x1 rib until last two stitches, P2tog. 60 sts.

Continue knitting in 1x1 rib until the cuff measures 4", or the desired length of the wearer. Bind off.

Repeat the above directions for the right cuff.

Finishing

Weave in any ends. With a yarn needle and yarn, close up any gaps around the seams and where the front band meets the neck. With a crochet hook and yarn, work a single crochet chain around the bottom of the sweater, starting at the beginning edge of the front band. This will give the edge a uniform appearance.

Due to the elastic nature of the yarn and the lace pattern, you may notice that the piece may have rebounded from the original blocking. To correct this, stretch the piece to the desired size and run a steam iron over it.

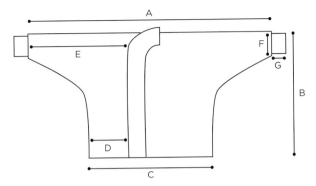

A 52 (54, 54, 56, 56)"
B 37" (all sizes)
C 18 (20, 22, 24, 26)"
D 6 (7, 8, 9, 10)"
E 22 (23, 24, 25, 26)"
F 12" (all sizes)
G 4" (all sizes)

Chart A

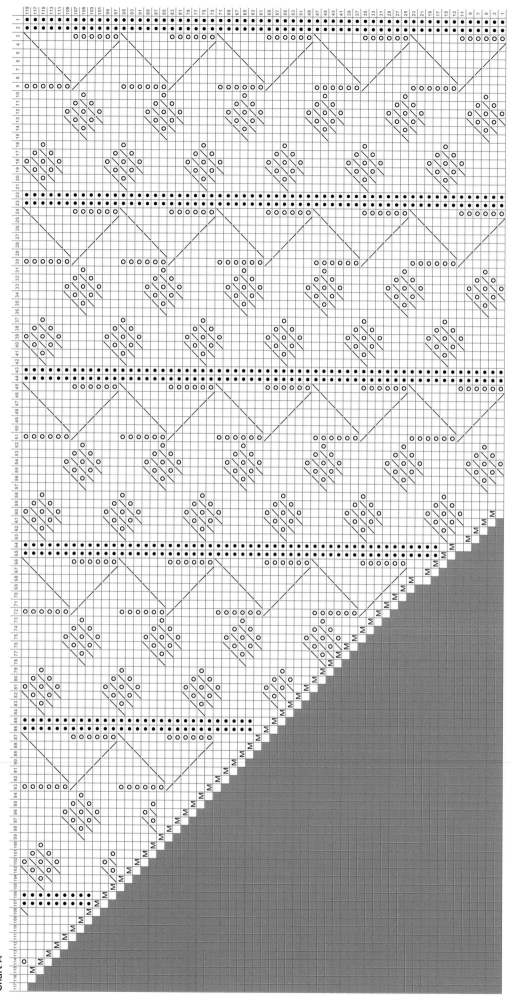

Chart B

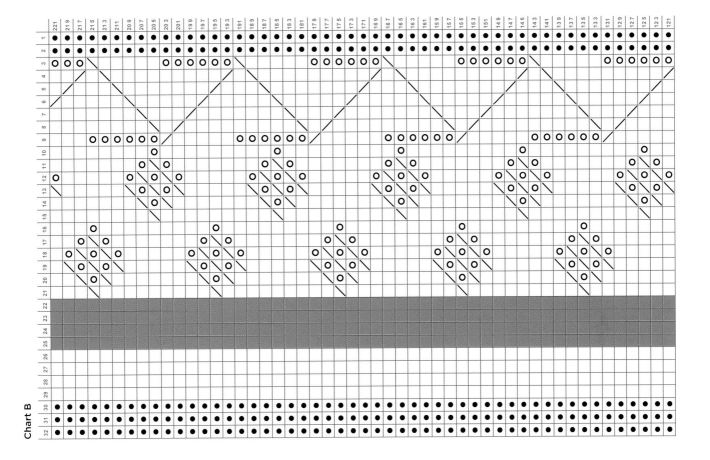

Legend

●	**purl**	purl stitch
○	**yo**	yarn over
╱	**ssk**	slip one stitch as if to knit, slip another stitch as if to knit. Insert left-hand needle into front of these 2 stitches and knit them together
☐	**knit**	knit stitch
╲	**k2tog**	knit two stitches together as one stitch
▓	**no stitch**	placeholder - no stitch made.
M	**make one**	Make one by lifting strand in between stitch just worked adn the next stitch, knit into back of this thread

Chart C

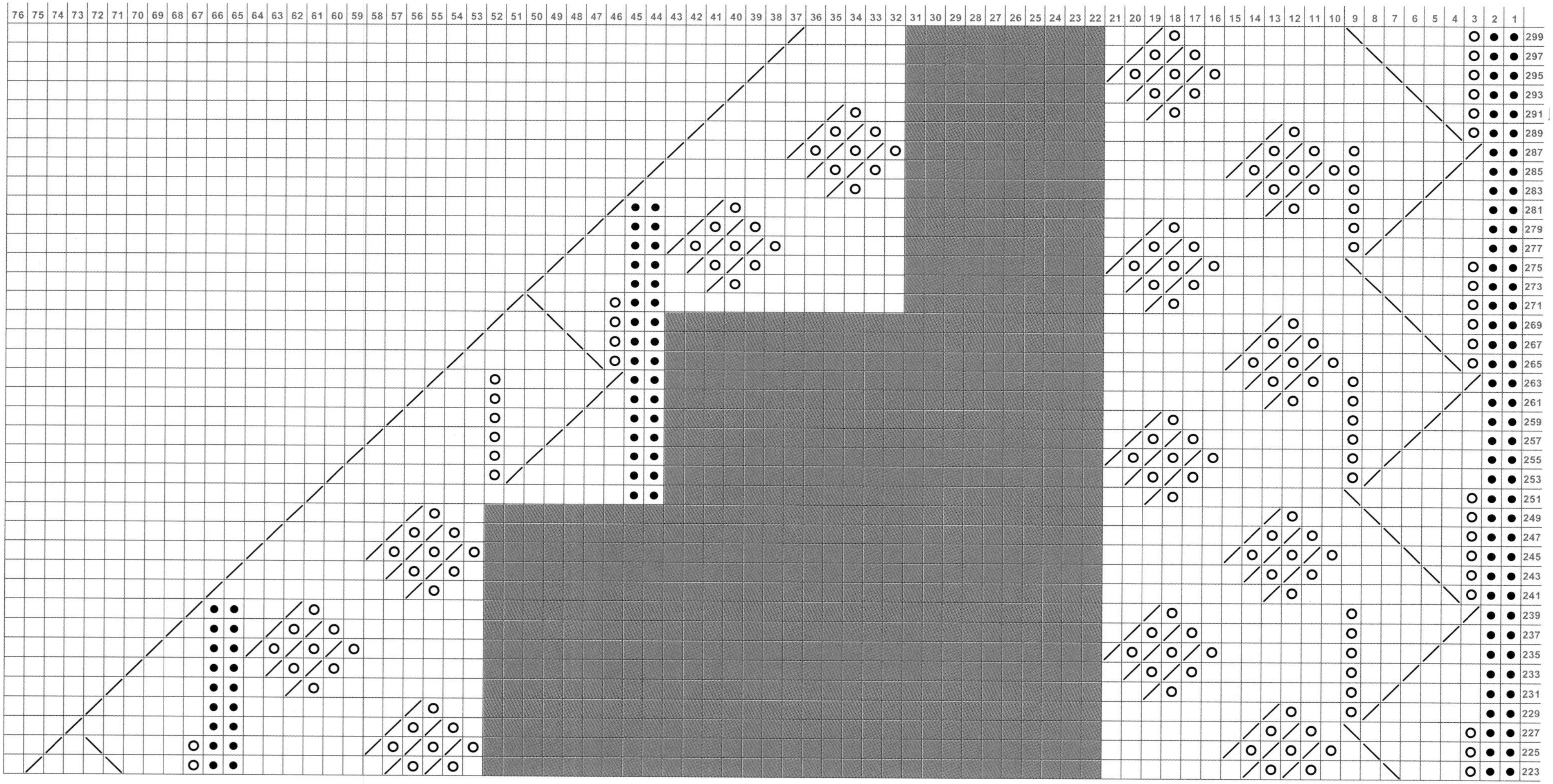

Chart C, continued

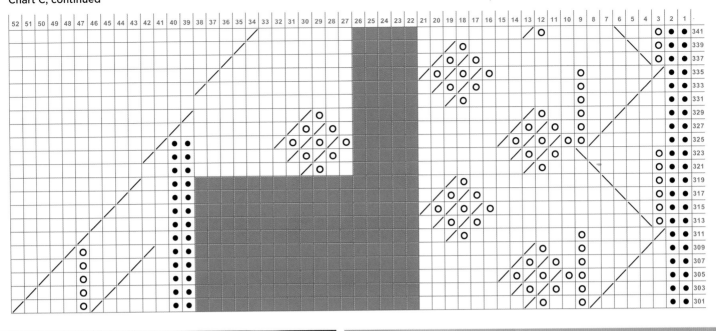

KAYDEN TANK

by Quenna Lee

FINISHED MEASUREMENTS

33.25 (35, 37, 40, 43, 46.75, 51, 54.75, 59)″
finished bust measurement; garment is
means to be worn with 1″ of ease

YARN

Knit Picks Lindy Chain (70% Linen, 30%
Pima Cotton; 180 yards/50g): Navy 26452,
4 (4, 4, 4, 5, 5, 5, 6, 6) balls

NEEDLES

US 4 (3.5mm) 24″ or longer circular needle
depending on garment size, plus spare
needle for 3-Needle BO, or size to obtain
gauge

NOTIONS

Scrap Yarn or Stitch Holder
Stitch Markers, 1 of them removable
Yarn Needle

GAUGE

24 sts and 30 rows = 4″ over St st worked in
the round, blocked.
24 sts and 32 rows = 4″ over St st worked in
the round, unblocked

Kayden Tank

Notes:

This tank has a split hem that is worked back and forth before being joined to work in the round. At the underarm, the body is divided into front and back and worked back and forth. A garter edging is worked simultaneously with the front and back.

Since the recommended yarn relaxes after blocking, the unblocked row gauge is used to determine vertical measurements in the pattern. If the row gauge remains constant after blocking, use the blocked measurements in schematic.

If unable to achieve the unblocked row gauge, determine the vertical measurements using the following calculation: Unblocked vertical measurement = (blocked/final measurement multiplied by blocked row gauge per inch) divided by unblocked row gauge per inch.

Garter Rib Stitch (over an even number of sts, worked flat or in the rnd):
Row/Rnd 1: Knit.
Row/Rnd 2: P1, K1.
Rep Rows/Rnds 1–2 for pat.

Eyelet Rib Stitch (worked in the rnd over 4 sts):
Rnd 1: P1, yo, ssk, P1.
Rnd 2: P1, K2, P1.
Rnd 3: P1, k2tog, yo, P1.
Rnd 4: Rep Rnd 2.
Rep Rnds 1–4 for pat.

Eyelet Rib Stitch (worked flat over 4 sts):
Row 1 (RS): P1, yo, ssk, P1.
Row 2 (WS): K1, P2, K1.
Row 3: P1, k2tog, yo, P1.
Row 4: Rep Row 2.
Rep Rows 1–4 for pat.

Vertical Gather (worked over 1 st):
With right needle pick up the 7th st directly below the next st and place on left needle, k2tog with next st.

Wrap & Turn (W&T)
Work until the stitch to be wrapped. If knitting: Bring yarn to the front of the work, slip next st as if to purl, return the yarn to the back; turn work and slip wrapped st onto RH needle. Continue across row. If purling: Bring yarn to the back of the work, slip next st as if to purl, return the yarn to the front; turn work and slip wrapped st onto RH needle. Continue across row.
Picking up wraps: Work to the wrapped st. If knitting, insert the RH needle under the wrap(s), then through the wrapped st kwise. Knit the wrap(s) together with the wrapped st. If purling, slip the wrapped st pwise onto the RH needle, and use the LH needle to lift the wrap(s) and place them on the RH needle. Slip wrap(s) and unworked st back to LH needle; purl all together through the back loop.

M1L (Make 1 Left-leaning stitch): PU the bar between st just worked and next st and place on LH needle as a regular stitch; knit through the back loop.

M1R (Make 1 Right-leaning stitch): PU the bar between st just worked and next st and place on LH needle backwards (incorrect stitch mount). Knit through the front loop.

3-Needle BO
* Hold the two pieces of knitting together with the points facing to the right. Insert a third needle into the first st on each of the needles Kwise, starting with the front needle. Work a knit st, pulling the loop through both of the sts you've inserted the third needle through. After pulling the loop through, sl the first st off of each of the needles. Repeat from *. Pass the first finished st over the second and off of the needle.

DIRECTIONS
Body
Hem

CO 100 (106, 112, 120, 130, 142, 154, 166, 178) sts, drop yarn. With second ball of yarn, CO 100 (106, 112, 120, 130, 142, 154, 166, 178) sts. 200 (212, 224, 240, 260, 284, 308, 332, 356) sts. Work Garter Rib across both pieces for 8 (8, 8, 8, 8, 10, 10, 10, 10) rows, ending after WS row. Cut yarn from second ball. PM and join pieces to begin working in the rnd.

RS: Continue Garter Rib for 10 (12, 14, 14, 16, 20, 22, 24, 26) sts, work Eyelet Rib for 4 sts, PM, work St st for 71 (75, 75, 83, 91, 95, 101, 111, 117) sts, PM, work Eyelet Rib for 4 sts, continue Garter Rib for 21 (23, 29, 29, 31, 39, 45, 47, 53) sts, work Eyelet Rib for 4 sts, PM, work St st for 71 (75, 75, 83, 91, 95, 101, 111, 117) sts, PM, work Eyelet Rib for 4 sts, continue Garter Rib for 11 (11, 15, 15, 15, 19, 23, 23, 27) sts.
Work in pat for 1 rnd.

Waist Shaping

Dec Rnd: *Continue in pat to next marker, SM, k2tog, work to 2 sts before next marker, ssk, SM, rep from * once more, work to end of rnd. 4 sts dec.
Rep Dec Rnd every 6 (6, 6, 7, 6, 6, 7, 7, 7)th rnd 5 more times. 176 (188, 200, 216, 236, 260, 284, 308, 332) sts rem.
Work in pat until piece measures 5.75 (5.75, 5.75, 6.25, 6, 6.25, 6.5, 6.5, 6.5)" unblocked from CO, ending after Row 2 of Garter Rib.

Bust Shaping

Inc Rnd: *Continue in pat to next marker, SM, M1L, work to next marker, M1R, SM, rep from * once more, work to end of rnd. 4 sts inc.
Rep Inc Rnd every 9 (9, 8, 8, 8, 8, 8, 8, 8)th rnd 5 more times. 200 (212, 224, 240, 260, 284, 308, 332, 356) sts.
Work in pat until piece measures 13.75 (13.5, 13.25, 13.5, 13.25, 13.25, 13.75, 13.75, 13.75)" unblocked from CO, ending after Row 2 of Garter Rib.

Divide Front and Back

Divide for armholes: Place last 100 (106, 112, 120, 130, 142, 154, 166, 178) sts on a holder for front. 100 (106, 112, 120, 130, 142, 154, 166, 178) sts on needle for back.

Back
Armhole Shaping

While working in pat, BO 5 (6, 6, 7, 8, 10, 11, 12, 13) sts at beginning of next 2 rows. BO 3 (3, 3, 4, 4, 5, 6, 6, 7) sts at the beginning of next 4 rows. 78 (82, 88, 90, 98, 102, 108, 118, 124) sts.

Dec Row (RS): Sl 1 st, K2, k2tog, K to last 5 sts, ssk, K3. 2 sts dec.
Next Row (WS): Sl 1 st, K2, P to last 3 sts, K3.

Rep last 2 rows 4 (5, 6, 6, 8, 8, 9, 10, 11) more times. 68 (70, 74, 76, 80, 84, 88, 96, 100) sts.
Work in pat until armhole measures 4.75 (5, 5, 5, 5.5, 5.5, 5.75, 6, 6.25)" unblocked, ending after a WS row.

Neck Edging
Row 1 (RS): Sl 1 st, K.
Row 2 (WS): Sl 1 st, K2, P11 (11, 13, 13, 13, 15, 15, 15, 17), K40 (42, 42, 44, 48, 48, 52, 60, 60), P11 (11, 13, 13, 13, 15, 15, 15, 17) sts, K3.
Work last 2 rows one more time. Armhole should measure 5 (5.25, 5.25, 5.25, 5.75, 5.75, 6, 6.25, 6.5)" unblocked.

Neck Shaping
On the RS, while continuing in pat, work 17 (17, 19, 19, 19, 21, 21, 21, 23) right shoulder sts and place on holder. Drop yarn. Join 2nd ball of yarn and BO 34 (36, 36, 38, 42, 42, 46, 54, 54) sts, work 17 (17, 19, 19, 19, 21, 21, 21, 23) left shoulder sts to the end.
Work in pat for 1 WS row.

Left Shoulder Shaping
Row 1 (RS): Sl 1 st, K2, k2tog, K to end. 1 st dec.
Row 2 (WS): Sl 1 st, K2, P to last 3 sts, K3.
Rep last 2 rows 2 more times. 14 (14, 16, 16, 16, 18, 18, 18, 20) sts.
Work in pat until armhole measures 6.25 (6.5, 6.75, 7, 7.5, 7.75, 8.25, 8.75, 9.25)" unblocked, ending after a WS row.

Short Row 1 (RS): While continuing in pat, work 8 (8, 10, 10, 10, 12, 12, 12, 12) sts, W&T.
Work in pat 1 WS row.

Short Row 2 (RS): While continuing in pat, work 4 (4, 5, 5, 5, 6, 6, 6, 6) sts, W&T.
Work in pat 1 WS row.

Next Row (RS): Work in pat, knitting wraps together with wrapped sts.
Work in pat for 3 rows.
Break yarn, leaving a 20" tail. Place sts on holder.

Right Shoulder Shaping
Transfer right shoulder sts to needle, ready to work a WS row. Sl 1 st, K2, P to last 3 sts, K3.

Shoulder Shaping
Row 1 (RS): Sl 1 st, K to last 5 sts, ssk, K3.
Row 2 (WS): Sl 1 st, K2, P to last 3 sts, K3.
Rep last 2 rows 2 more times. 14 (14, 16, 16, 16, 18, 18, 18, 20) sts.
Work in pat until armhole measures 6.25 (6.5, 6.75, 7, 7.5, 7.75, 8.25, 8.75, 9.25)" unblocked, ending after a RS row.
Short Row 1 (WS): While continuing, in pat work 8 (8, 10, 10, 10, 12, 12, 12, 12) sts, W&T.
Work in pat 1 RS row.
Short Row 2 (WS): While continuing in pat, work 4 (4, 5, 5, 5, 6, 6, 6, 6) sts, W&T.
Work in pat 1 RS row.
Next Row (WS): Work in pat, purling wraps together with wrapped sts.
Work in pat for 2 rows.
Break yarn, leaving a 20" tail. Place sts on holder.

Front
Armhole Shaping
Note: Vertical Gathers will begin before armhole shaping is completed. PLEASE READ AHEAD through both sections before proceeding.

Transfer front sts to needle and join yarn at the left shoulder edge, ready to work a RS row. Place a removable marker after 41 (44, 47, 51, 53, 59, 65, 71, 77) sts.
While working in pat, BO 5 (6, 6, 7, 8, 10, 11, 12, 13) sts at beginning of next 2 rows. BO 3 (3, 3, 4, 4, 4, 5, 6, 6, 7) sts at the beginning of next 4 rows. 78 (82, 88, 90, 98, 102, 108, 118, 124) sts.
Dec Row (RS): Sl 1 st, K2, k2tog, K to last 5 sts, ssk, K3. 2 sts dec.
Dec Row (WS): Sl 1 st, K2, P to last 3 sts, K3.
Rep last 2 rows 4 (5, 6, 6, 8, 8, 9, 10, 11) more times. 68 (70, 74, 76, 80, 84, 88, 96, 100) sts.
WHILE WORKING THE DEC ROWS, begin Vertical Gathers, when armhole measures 1.25 (1.5, 1.5, 1.5, 2, 2, 2.25, 2.5, 2.75)" unblocked, ending after a WS row.

Vertical Gathers
Set Up Row (RS): Work to removable marker, SM, K6 (6, 6, 6, 8, 8, 8, 8, 8), work Vertical Gather, K5 (5, 5, 5, 7, 7, 7, 7, 7), work Vertical Gather, work to end of row. Work in pat for 7 rows.

Vertical Gather Row (RS): Work to marker, SM, *work Vertical Gather, K5 (5, 5, 5, 7, 7, 7, 7, 7), rep from * twice, K5 (5, 5, 5, 7, 7, 7, 7, 7), work Vertical Gather, work to end of row.
Work Vertical Gather Row every 8th row 1 more time.
Work in pat 1 WS row.

Neck Edging (RS): Sl 1 st, K to end.
Next Row (WS): Sl 1 st, K2, P11 (11, 13, 13, 13, 15, 15, 15, 17), K40 (42, 42, 44, 48, 48, 52, 60, 60), P11 (11, 13, 13, 13, 15, 15, 15, 17) sts, K3.
Work last 2 rows one more time. Armhole should measure 3 (3.25, 3.25, 3.25, 3.75, 4, 4.25, 4.5, 4.75)" unblocked.

Neck Shaping
On the RS, while continuing in pat, work 17 (17, 19, 19, 19, 21, 21, 21, 23) left shoulder sts and place on holder. Drop yarn. Join 2nd ball of yarn and BO 34 (36, 36, 38, 42, 42, 46, 54, 54) sts, work 17 (17, 19, 19, 19, 21, 21, 21, 23) right shoulder sts to the end. Work in pat for 1 WS row.

Right Shoulder Shaping
Follow directions for back left shoulder.

Left Shoulder Shaping
Follow directions for back right shoulder.

Finishing
With RS facing each other, seam shoulders using 3-Needle BO.
Weave in ends and block to measurements.

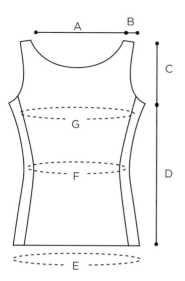

A 5.75 (6, 6, 6.25, 7, 7, 7.5, 9, 9)"
B 2.75 (2.75, 3, 3, 3, 3.5, 3.5, 3.5, 3.75)"
C 7.75 (8, 8.25, 8.5, 9, 9.25, 9.75, 10.25, 10.75)"
D 14.75 (14.5, 14.25, 14.5, 14.5, 14, 14.25, 14.75, 14.75, 14.75)"
E 33.25 (35.25, 37.25, 40, 43.25, 47.25, 51.25, 55.25, 59.25)"
F 29.25 (31.25, 33.25, 36, 39.25, 43.25, 47.25, 51.25, 55.25)"
G 33.25 (35.25, 37.25, 40, .43.25, 47.25, 51.245, 55.25, 59.25)"

DAISIES CARDIGAN

by Erica Jackofsky

FINISHED MEASUREMENTS

32 (37, 40, 43, 48, 52, 56, 59, 63)" finished bust measurement; garment is meant to be worn with approximately 4" of positive ease

YARN

Knit Picks Shine Sport (60% Pima Cotton, 40% Modal; 110 yards/50g): Macaw 25343, 8 (8, 9, 11, 12, 13, 14, 15, 17) balls

NEEDLES

US 4 (3.5mm) 24-32" circular needle, or size to obtain gauge
US 4 (3.5mm) DPNs, 24" circular needles for two circulars technique, or one 32" or longer circular needle for Magic Loop technique, or size to obtain gauge

US 6 (4mm) spare needle for BO, or 1-2 sizes larger than gauge needle (optional)

NOTIONS

Yarn Needle
8 Stitch Markers
Scrap Yarn or Stitch Holder

GAUGE

22 sts and 32 rows = 4" in Stockinette st, blocked

Daisies Cardigan

Notes:

This cardigan combines comfort and style, with a relaxed fit and gorgeous textured stitches. Easy to pull on over a dress or a long-sleeve shirt, it's a versatile piece with subtle shaping and interesting details. All references to Right and Left are as worn, unless otherwise noted.

The Main Body through row 32 (40, 44, 48, 56, 60, 64, 68, 72) can be confusing when just reading the pattern, however, once you get going you should start to see the pattern emerging. On each side of the cardigan there is a pyramid pattern of Daisy stitches. Each time you work a RS row you will work one less repeat of the 4-stitch Daisy pattern repeat. Flanking the daisy pattern is a slanting "yo, SM, ssk" on the right and "k2tog, SM, yo" on the left. To the right and left of the pyramid (between the ribbing and yo) is all Stockinette st (K on RS rows, P on WS rows).

Daisy Stitch (multiple of 4 sts)
* K3tog, but do not remove st from left needle, yo on right needle, K3tog again into same 3 sts and drop sts from left needle, P1; repeat from * over required sts.

2x2 Ribbing (worked flat over a multiple of 4 plus 2 stitches)
Row 1: K2, *P2, K2; rep from * to end of row.
Row 2: P2, *K2, P2; rep from * to end of row.
Rep Rows 1 and 2 for pat.

Slip, Purl 2 Together, Pass Slip Stitch Over (SP2P)
Slip first st as if to purl, purl 2 sts together, pass the slipped st over the p2tog. 2 sts dec.

Knit 2 Together Stretchy Bind Off
Use a needle 1 to 2 sizes larger than working needle.
K2, *place 2 sts back on left needle and knit together through the back loops. 1 stitch remains on right needle. K1; repeat from * until all sts have been bound off. Fasten off last st.

Make 1 (M1)
PU a st from the row below the working st on the LH needle. Knit into this st. 1 st inc.

M1L (Make 1 Left-leaning stitch)
PU the bar between st just worked and next st and place on LH needle mounted as a regular knit stitch; knit through the back of the loop.

M1R (Make 1 Right-leaning stitch)
PU the bar between st just worked and next st and place on LH needle backwards (incorrect stitch mount). Knit through the front of the loop.

Sewn Bind Off
Cut yarn at least 3 times longer than circumference to be bound off. Thread a yarn needle.
Step 1: Insert yarn needle and pull yarn through first 2 sts on left needle as if to purl.
Step 2: Insert yarn needle kwise through first st on left needle. Pull yarn through and remove first st from needle. One st BO.
Repeat steps 1 and 2 until all sts have been bound off.

DIRECTIONS
Body
Cast on 182 (214, 230, 246, 278, 294, 322, 338, 358) sts.
Work in 2x2 Ribbing for 2″ ending with a RS row.

Increase Row (WS): *P2, K2* 3 (3, 3, 3, 3, 3, 4, 4, 4) times, PM to note ribbed band, *P2, K2* 9 (11, 12, 13, 15, 16, 17, 18, 19) times, M1, *P2, K2* 9 (11, 12, 13, 15, 16, 17, 18, 19) times, PM to note center back section, *P2, K2* 3 (3, 3, 3, 3, 3, 4, 4, 5) times, P2, PM to note end of center back section, *K2, P2* 9 (11, 12, 13, 15, 16, 17, 18, 19) times, M1, *K2, P2* 9 (11, 12, 13, 15, 16, 17, 18, 19) times, PM to note ribbed band, *K2, P2* 3 (3, 3, 3, 3, 3, 4, 4, 4) times. 2 sts inc. 184 (216, 232, 248, 280, 296, 324, 340, 360) sts.

Establish Daisy Stitch Pattern
Row 1 (RS): *K2, P2* 3 (3, 3, 3, 3, 3, 4, 4, 4) times, SM, yo, PM, ssk, P1, work 17 (21, 23, 25, 29, 31, 33, 35, 37) repeats of Daisy Stitch, k2tog, PM, yo, SM, *K2, P2* 3 (3, 3, 3, 3, 3, 4, 4, 5) times, K2, SM, yo, PM, ssk, P1, work 17 (21, 23, 25, 29, 31, 33, 35, 37) repeats of Daisy Stitch, k2tog, PM, yo, SM, *P2, K2* 3 (3, 3, 3, 3, 3, 4, 4, 4) times.
Row 2 (WS): *P2, K2* 3 (3, 3, 3, 3, 3, 4, 4, 4) times, SM, P1, yo, SM, P2TOG, P to 2 sts before next marker, SSP, SM, yo, P1, SM, *P2, K2* 3 (3, 3, 3, 3, 3, 4, 4, 5) times, P2, SM, P1, yo, SM, P2TOG, P to 2 sts before next marker, SSP, SM, yo, P1, SM, *K2, P2* 3 (3, 3, 3, 3, 3, 4, 4, 4) times.

Rows 3 through 32 (40, 44, 48, 56, 60, 64, 68, 72)
Odd Numbered Rows (RS): *Work in established 2x2 ribbing to marker, SM, K to next marker, yo, SM, ssk, P1, work in Daisy Stitch to 2 sts before next marker, k2tog, SM, yo, K to marker, SM, * repeat from * once more, work in established 2x2 ribbing to end of row.
Even Numbered Rows (WS): *Work in established 2x2 ribbing to marker, SM, P to next marker, yo, SM, P2TOG, P to 2 sts before next marker, SSP, SM, yo, P to marker, SM; repeat from * once more, work in established 2x2 ribbing to end of row.
Work these two rows another 14 (18, 20, 22, 26, 28, 30, 32, 34) times.

Row 33 (41, 45, 49, 57, 61, 65, 69, 73) (RS): *Work in established 2x2 ribbing to marker, SM, K to next marker, yo, SM, ssk, P1, work in Daisy Stitch to 2 sts before next marker, k2tog, SM, yo, K to marker, SM, repeat from * once more, work in established 2x2 ribbing to end of row.
Row 34 (42, 46, 50, 58, 62, 66, 70, 74) (WS): *Work in established 2x2 ribbing to marker, SM, P to next marker, yo, SM, P2TOG, P3, SSP, SM, yo, P to marker, SM; repeat from * once more, work in established 2x2 ribbing to end of row.
Row 35 (43, 47, 51, 59, 63, 67, 71, 75) (RS): *Work in established 2x2 ribbing to marker, SM, K to next marker, yo, SM, ssk, K1, k2tog, SM, yo, K to marker, SM, repeat from * once more, work in established 2x2 ribbing to end of row.
Row 36 (44, 48, 52, 60, 64, 68, 72, 76) (WS): *Work in established 2x2 ribbing to marker, SM, P to next marker, yo, SM, SP2P, SM, yo, P to next marker, SM; repeat from * once more, work in established 2x2 ribbing to end of row.

Decrease Section
The Daisies pattern is now complete, those sts will be worked in St st going forward.

Row 1 (RS): Work as established to marker, SM, K to next ribbed section, SM, work in 2x2 ribbing, SM, K to last marker, SM, work as established to end.

Row 2 (WS): Work as established to marker, SM, P to next ribbed section, SM, work in 2x2 ribbing, SM, P to last marker, work as established to end.

Decrease Row (RS): Work as established to marker, SM, K to 2 sts before next marker, k2tog, SM, K1, SM, K to 2 sts before next marker, k2tog, SM, work in established 2x2 ribbing to next marker, SM, ssk, K to next marker, SM, K1, SM, ssk, K to next marker, SM, work as established to end. 4 sts dec.

Work Decrease Row every 12th (10th, 10th, 10th, 8th, 8th, 6th, 6th, 6th) row a total of 5 (5, 5, 5, 5, 5, 6, 6, 6) times – 164 (196, 212, 228, 260, 276, 300, 316, 336) sts.

Work even in pat until piece measures 15.5 (16, 16, 16.5, 16.5, 17, 17, 17.5, 17.5)″ from cast on edge, ending on a WS row.

Shape Upper Body

At this point the fronts and back will be worked separately through the remainder of the piece. You should be ready to work a RS row before proceeding.

Right Front

Sleeve Increases and Neckline shaping occur simultaneously, read through both sections before proceeding.

Row 1 (RS): *K2, P2* 3 (3, 3, 3, 3, 3, 4, 4, 4) times, SM, K31 (39, 43, 47, 55, 59, 67, 71, 75). These 43 (51, 55, 59, 67, 71, 83, 87, 91) sts create the right front. Place all remaining sts on scrap yarn or stitch holder and set aside.

Row 2 (WS): Purl to marker, SM, work as established to end.

Sleeve Increases

Beginning immediately and working in established pat, M1 at each armhole (1 st in from the edge) on this row and then every 5 (6, 6, 6, 7, 6, 6, 6) rows 3 (9, 5, 1, 1, 7, 11, 7, 7) times, and then every 6 (0, 7, 7, 7, 8, 0, 7, 7) rows 6 (0, 4, 8, 8, 2, 0, 4, 4) times. 10 (10, 10, 10, 10, 10, 12, 12, 12) sts inc at armhole edge.
Work even in established pat until piece measures 7 (7.5, 8, 8.5, 8.5, 9, 9, 9.5, 9.5)″ from armhole split before beginning shoulder shaping.

Shape Shoulder: BO 4 (5, 6, 6, 7, 8, 10, 9, 11) sts at armhole edge 7 (7, 3, 7, 7, 2, 2, 6, 2) times, then BO 3 (4, 5, 5, 6, 7, 8, 9, 9) sts 1 (1, 5, 1, 1, 6, 6, 2, 6) times. 12 (12, 12, 12, 12, 12, 16, 16, 16) sts rem after Shape Shoulder and Neckline Shaping are complete.
Work even in 2x2 ribbing for 3 (3, 3, 3, 3, 3.25, 3.25, 3.25, 3.5)″ for collar extension. Bind off.

Neckline Shaping

AT THE SAME TIME, begin neckline shaping after front piece measures 1″ (8 rows).

Neckline Decrease Row (RS): Work as established to marker, SM, K1, ssk, knit to end. 1 st dec.

Neckline Decrease Row (WS): Purl to 3 sts before marker, SSP, P1, SM, work as established to end. 1 st dec.

Work Neckline Decrease Row (RS or WS as appropriate) every 5 (6, 6, 6, 6, 6, 6, 7, 7) rows 8 (8, 6, 10, 10, 9, 9, 2, 2) times, then every

5 (5, 5, 0, 0, 5, 5, 6, 6) rows 2 (2, 4, 0, 0, 2, 2, 9, 9) times. 10 (10, 10, 10, 10, 11, 11, 11, 11) sts dec at neck.

Left Front

Place 43 (51, 55, 59, 67, 71, 83, 87, 91) sts for Left Front on working needle and attach yarn with RS facing.

Row 1 (RS): K31 (39, 43, 47, 55, 59, 67, 71, 75) sts, SM, work as established to end of row.

Row 2 (WS): Work as established to marker, SM, P to end of row.

Sleeve Increases

Beginning immediately and working in established pat, M1 at each armhole (1 st in from the edge) on this row and then every 5 (6, 6, 6, 7, 6, 6, 6) rows 3 (9, 5, 1, 1, 7, 11, 7, 7) times and then every 6 (0, 7, 7, 7, 8, 0, 7, 7) rows 6 (0, 4, 8, 8, 2, 0, 4, 4) times. 10 (10, 10, 10, 10, 10, 12, 12, 12) sts inc at armhole edge.
Work even in established pat until piece measures 7 (7.5, 8, 8.5, 8.5, 9, 9, 9.5, 9.5)″ from armhole split before beginning shoulder shaping.

Shape Shoulder: BO 4 (5, 6, 6, 7, 8, 10, 9, 11) sts at armhole edge 7 (7, 3, 7, 7, 2, 2, 6, 2) times, then BO 3 (4, 5, 5, 6, 7, 8, 9, 9) sts 1 (1, 5, 1, 1, 6, 6, 2, 6) times. 12 (12, 12, 12, 12, 12, 16, 16, 16) sts rem after Shape Shoulder and Neckline Shaping are complete.
Work even in 2x2 ribbing for 3 (3, 3, 3, 3, 3.25, 3.25, 3.25, 3.5)″ for collar extension.
Bind off.

Shape Neckline

AT THE SAME TIME begin neckline shaping after front piece measures 1″ (8 rows).

Neckline Decrease Row (RS): K to 3 sts before marker, K2tog, K1, SM, work as established to end.

Neckline Decrease Row (WS): Work as established to 1st marker, SM, P1, P2TOG, P to end of row.
Work Neckline Decrease Row (RS or WS as appropriate) every 5 (6, 6, 6, 6, 6, 6, 7, 7) rows 8 (8, 6, 10, 10, 9, 9, 2, 2) times, then every 5 (5, 5, 0, 0, 5, 5, 6, 6) rows 2 (2, 4, 0, 0, 2, 2, 9, 9) times. 10 (10, 10, 10, 10, 11, 11, 11, 11) sts dec at neck.

Back

Place rem 78 (94, 102, 110, 126, 134, 134, 142, 154) sts for back on working needle and attach yarn with RS facing.

Row 1 (RS): BO 1 st, K to marker, SM, *K2, P2* 3 (3, 3, 3, 3, 3, 4, 4, 5) times, K2, SM, K to end. 77 (93, 101, 109, 125, 133, 133, 141, 153) sts.

Row 2 (WS): BO 1 st, P to marker, SM, *P2, K2* 3 (3, 3, 3, 3, 3, 4, 4, 5) times, P2, SM, purl to end. 76 (92, 100, 108, 124, 132, 132, 140, 152) sts.

Sleeve Increases

Increase Row (RS and WS): Work 2 sts as established, M1R, work to marker, SM, work established ribbing, SM, work to 2 sts before end, M1L, work 2 sts as established. 2 sts inc.
Beginning immediately and working in established pat, increase 1 st at each armhole edge as noted in the Increase Row on this row and then every 5 (6, 6, 6, 7, 6, 6, 6) rows 3 (9, 5, 1, 1, 7, 11, 7, 7) times and then every 6 (0, 7, 7, 7, 8, 0, 7, 7) rows 6 (0, 4, 8, 8, 2, 0,

4, 4) times – 20 (20, 20, 20, 20, 20, 24, 24, 24) sts inc at armhole edges. 96 (112, 120, 128, 144, 152, 156, 164, 176) sts.

Work even in established pat until piece measures 7 (7.5, 8, 8.5, 8.5, 9, 9, 9.5, 9.5)" from armhole split before beginning shoulder shaping to match fronts.

Shape Shoulder: BO 4 (5, 6, 6, 7, 8, 10, 9, 11) sts at armhole edge 14 (14, 6, 14, 14, 4, 4, 12, 4) times, then 3 (4, 5, 5, 6, 7, 8, 9, 9) sts 2 (2, 10, 2, 2, 12, 12, 4, 12) times.

Bind off remaining 34 (34, 34, 34, 34, 36, 20, 20, 24) sts for back neck.

Finishing

Sew shoulder seams. Sew bound off ends of ribbed front band/collar. Sew edges of ribbed collar extensions to the back of neck aligning the seam with the center back of garment.

Armhole Edging: With RS facing, PU and K 76 (84, 88, 96, 96, 100, 100, 104, 104) sts evenly spaced around arm opening. Work in 2x2 ribbing for 1". Bind off using stretchy bind off such as the Knit 2 Together Stretchy Bind Off or Sewn Bind Off (see Notes).

Weave in ends and block to dimensions.

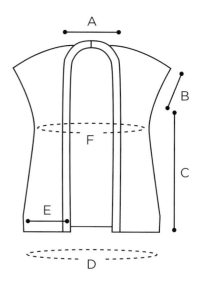

A   6 (6, 6, 6, 6, 6.5, 6.5, 6.5, 7.25)"
B   7 (7.5, 8, 8.5, 8.5, 9, 9, 9.5, 9.5)"
C   15.5 (16, 16, 16.5, 16.5, 17, 17, 17.5, 17.5)"
D   31 (37, 40, 43, 48, 52, 56, 59, 63)"
E   8.75 (10, 11, 11.5, 13, 14, 15, 16, 16.75)"
F   28 (33.5, 36, 39, 45, 48, 52, 55, 60)"

NAMASTE TOP

by Katy Banks

FINISHED MEASUREMENTS

30 (34, 38, 42, 46.25, 50.25, 54.25, 58.25, 62.25)" finished bust measurement; garment is meant to be worn with 2" of negative ease

YARN

Knit Picks Swish DK (100% Superwash Merino Wool; 123 yards/50g): C1 Dusk 24053 4 (4, 5, 5, 6, 7, 8, 8) balls; C2 White 24064 3 (4, 4, 5, 5, 6, 6, 7, 7) balls; C3 Carnation 24962 1 (1, 1, 1, 1, 2, 2, 2) balls

NEEDLES

US 6 (4mm) 24" or longer circular needle, the length of the cable should be shorter than your desired finished bust

measurement, plus additional needle(s) of the same size for using two circulars technique, or Magic Loop technique, or DPNs, or size to obtain gauge

NOTIONS

Yarn Needle
Stitch Markers
Scrap Yarn or Stitch Holder
Crochet Hook and Smooth Waste Yarn, or as preferred for Provisional CO

GAUGE

20 sts and 24 rows = 4" in St st, blocked
22 sts and 28 rows = 4" in Corrugated Rib blocked

Namaste Top

Notes:

This top is worked in an unusual manner to achieve stripes that travel in different and flattering ways. You begin part way down the yoke, working single row stripes in the round to reach the bottom. Then the front, back, and each sleeve are continued separately from the yoke and are worked back and forth down to the hem and cuff. The live sts are placed on hold while you pick up and knit the side and under arm panels and "seam" them using the 3-Needle Bind-Off. The hem, cuffs, and upper yoke are then each worked in a corrugated 1x1 rib. Throughout the piece, occasional stripes of contrasting color pop up to create contrast and flattering lines.

Single Row Stripes (worked flat over any number of sts)

Row 1: With C1, K to the end, do not turn.

Row 2: Slide the work to the other end of the needle, with C2 (or C3, if indicated), K to the end, turn.

Row 3: With C1, P to the end, do not turn.

Row 4: Slide the work to the other end of the needle, with C2 (or C3, if indicated), P to the end, turn.

Rep Rows 1-4 for pat.

Corrugated Ribbing (worked flat over an odd number of sts)

Row 1: With C1, *K1, sl1wyib, repeat from * to the last st, K1.

Row 2: Slide the work to the other end of the needle, with C2, *sl1wyib, P1, repeat from * to the last st, sl1wyib.

Row 3: With C1, *P1, sl1wyif, repeat from * to the last st, P1.

Row 4: Slide the work to the other end of the needle, with C2, *sl1wyif, K1, repeat from * to the last st, sl1wyif.

Rep Rows 1-4 for pat.

Corrugated Ribbing (in the round over an even number of sts)

Round 1: With C1, *K1, sl1wyib, repeat from * to the end of the round.

Round 2: With C2, *sl1wyib, P1, repeat from * to the end of the round.

Rep Rnds 1-2 for pat.

3-Needle Bind Off

*Hold the two pieces of knitting together with the points facing to the right. Insert a third needle into the first stitch on each of the needles Kwise, starting with the front needle. Work a knit st, pulling the loop through both of the sts you've inserted the third needle through. After pulling the loop through, sl the first st off of each of the needles. Repeat from *. Pass the first finished st over the second and off of the needle.

DIRECTIONS

Lower Yoke

With C3 and using a provisional cast on method, CO 144 (162, 180, 201, 213, 231, 252, 264, 282) sts. Break C3. Join to begin working in the round, being careful not to twist sts.

Establishing seamless striping

With C1, K 72 (81, 90, 100, 106, 115, 126, 132, 141). Drop C1, place marker for the beginning of the round and join C2, K 1 rnd. From here on, you will change colors every round, alternating C1 and C2. If necessary, tug a bit on the yarn before working the first st

of the round to ensure the stripes connect seamlessly with no jog. After you have worked 6 (6, 9, 12, 12, 14, 15, 15, 17) rnds, work an increase round as follows: * K3, yo, repeat from * to the end of the round. 192 (216, 240, 268, 284)(308, 336, 352, 376) sts on needle. In the next round, K all yo's tbl so they are twisted.

After you have worked 11 (12, 14, 14, 15, 15, 15, 17, 16) more rnds, work an increase round as follows: * K4, yo, repeat from * to the end of the round. 240 (270, 300, 335, 355, 385, 420, 440, 470) sts on needle. In the next round, K all yo's tbl so they are twisted. After you have worked 9 (12, 13, 13, 14, 15, 17, 18, 20) more rnds, increase 0 (2, 0, 1, 1, 3, 0, 0, 2) sts evenly across the next rnd.

Back

Keep the next 71 (79, 89, 99, 105, 115, 125, 131, 141) sts on needle, place the rem on scrap yarn or holder. Work flat in Single Row Stripes, continuing established stripe pattern from yoke. Contrast Stripes and Decreases are worked simultaneously, read through both sections before proceeding.

Contrast Stripes

Work C3 in place of a C2 stripe when the piece measures approximately 5" from bottom of the yoke, and again at 6" and at 7".

AT THE SAME TIME:

Work straight for 4".

Decrease 1 st at either end of the needle on every other row 9 (10, 10, 10, 10, 10, 13, 14, 14) times. 53 (59, 69, 79, 85, 95, 99, 103, 113) sts.

Work straight until piece measures 9" from bottom of the yoke. Increase 1 st at either end of the needle on every other row 13 (13, 13, 13, 13, 13, 13, 15, 16) times. 79 (85, 95, 105, 111, 121, 125, 133, 145) sts.

Work straight until piece measures 15 (15, 15, 15, 15, 16, 16, 16, 16)" from the bottom of the yoke. On the last row C3 is worked in place of C2. Place all sts on scrap yarn or holder.

Sleeves

From the bottom of the yoke, place the next 49 (57, 61, 69, 73, 79, 85, 89, 95) held sts on needle. Work flat in Single Row Stripes, continuing established stripe pattern from yoke.
Work straight for 1".
Contrast Stripes and Decreases are worked simultaneously, read through both sections before proceeding.

Contrast Stripes

Work C3 in place of a C2 stripe when the piece measures approximately 5" from bottom of the yoke, and again at 6" and at 7".

AT THE SAME TIME:

Decrease 1 st at either end of the needle every 6 (6, 6, 7, 6, 6, 6, 7) rows 8 (9, 9, 10, 10, 11, 11, 11, 11) times then work straight until the sleeve length is 9 (10.5, 11.25, 12.25, 13, 13.5, 13.5, 13.75, 14)" from the bottom of the yoke, ending with a C1 row. 33 (39, 43, 49, 53, 57, 63, 67, 73) sts. Place all sts on scrap yarn or holder.
Repeat for other sleeve beginning with the same number of held sts on the opposite side of the yoke.

From the bottom of the yoke, place rem 71 (79, 89, 99, 105, 115, 125, 131, 141) held sts on needle and work as for the back. 79 (85, 95, 105, 111, 121, 125, 133, 145) sts.

Side Panels

With RS facing you, spread a Sleeve away from the adjacent Front so the selvedge edges form one straight line. With C3, PU and K 120 (125, 125, 130, 139, 140, 140, 140, 150) sts along this edge between the held sleeve sts and bottom hem held sts. Work 6 (7, 7, 7, 10, 10, 10, 12, 12) rows of Single Row Stripes in C1 and C2, worked flat. Place these sts on spare needle.

Repeat this process for the other selvedge edge of the same Sleeve which will continue along the adjacent Back. "Seam" these two side panels with next color in sequence, using the 3-Needle bind-off technique, leaving the 10 sts along the bottom edge of the body open for side vent. Place all 20 of these side vent stitches on scrap yarn or stitch holder.

Repeat for the other side.

Upper Yoke

Carefully remove the provisional CO and place the live C3 sts on needle(s). 144 (162, 180, 201, 213, 231, 252, 264, 282) sts.

Set Up Rnd: Beginning where the CO sts were joined for working in the round, slip 5 (7, 7, 8, 8, 11, 10, 10, 13) sts from the right needle to the left needle. Effectively, you are moving the place where you will start working back these few stitches. Join C1.

ssk 0 (1, 0, 1, 1, 0, 0, 0, 1) time, Sssk 0 (0, 0, 0, 0, 1, 0, 0, 0) time, K39 (44, 51, 57, 59, 65, 71, 73, 79) sts for right sleeve, PM, K33 (36, 39, 43, 47, 49, 55, 59, 61) sts for back, PM, ssk 0 (1, 0, 0, 0, 1, 0 , 0, 1) time, K39 (44, 51, 57, 59, 65, 71, 73, 79) sts for left sleeve, PM, K33 (36, 39, 43, 47, 49, 55, 59, 61) sts for front, PM. 144 (160, 180, 200, 212, 228, 252, 264, 280) sts.

You have just marked the boundaries between the right sleeve, back, left sleeve, and front sections, respectively. Note that the sleeve sections are wider than the front/back sections. Examine the piece to ensure these sections are centered above their counterparts below the yoke.

From this point on, you will use a selection of three types of odd-numbered rnds (below) in Corrugated Ribbing. Notice that the decreases are slanted from the corners in toward the centers of the sleeve sections while the front and back sections remain straight.

0-st Decrease Rnd: With C1, Sl wyib any st that was worked in the previous row, K any st that was Sl in the previous row.

4-st Decrease Rnd: With C1, [ssk, *sl1 wyib, K1, repeat from * to 3 sts before marker, sl1 wyib, K2tog, SM, * Sl1 wyib, K1, repeat from * to 1 st before marker, Sl1 wyib, SM] twice.

8-st Decrease Rnd: With C1, [Sssk, *sl1 wyib, K1, repeat from * to 4 sts before marker, sl1 wyib, K3tog, SM, * Sl1 wyib, K1, repeat from * to 1 st before marker, Sl1 wyib, SM] twice.

All even numbered rnds will be worked as follows.

Even Numbered Rnd: With C2, P any st that was Sl in the previous row, Sl wyib any st that was worked in the previous row.

Rnd 1: Work an 4-st Decrease Rnd.

Rnd 3: Work an 0 (4, 4, 4, 4, 4, 4, 4, 8)-st Decrease Rnd.

Rnd 5: 4 (4, 4, 4, 4, 4, 4, 4, 8)-st Decrease Rnd.

Rnd 7: Repeat Rnd 3.

Rnd 9: Work an 4 (4, 4, 4, 4, 4, 4, 8, 8)-st Decrease Rnd.

Rnd 11: Work an 0 (4, 4, 4, 4, 4, 8, 8, 8)-st Decrease Rnd.

Rnd 13: Work an 4 (4, 4, 4, 4, 8, 8, 8, 8)-st Decrease Rnd.

Rnd 15: Repeat Rnd 13.

Rnd 17: Work an 4 (4, 4, 4, 8, 8, 8, 8, 8)-st Decrease Rnd.

Rnd 19: Repeat Rnd 17.

Rnd 21: Repeat Rnd 17.

Rnd 23: Work an 4 (4, 4, 8, 8, 8, 8, 8)-st Decrease Rnd.

Rnd 25: Work an 4 (4, 8, 8, 8, 8, 8, 8)-st Decrease Rnd.

Rnd 27: Repeat Rnd 25.

Rnd 29: Repeat Rnd 25.

Rnd 31: Work an 4 (4, 8, 8, 8, 8, 8, 8)-st Decrease Rnd.

Rnd 33: Repeat Rnd 31.

Rnd 35: Repeat Rnd 31.

Use C3 to BO rem 84 (88, 96, 104, 112, 116, 128, 136, 140) sts.

Hems

Return to the bottom edge of the Back piece. With RS facing, join C2 and PU and K 5 (6, 6, 6, 8, 8, 8, 10, 10) sts along the lower edge of one side panel, K the held sts, PU and K the same number of sts along the lower edge of the other side panel. 89 (97, 107, 117, 127, 137, 141, 153, 165) sts.

Slide work to the opposite end of the needle. Work flat in Corrugated Rib for 2". Use C3 to BO.

Repeat for Front Hem.

Side Slits

With C3 and beginning at the bottom corner of one hem, pickup and K 10 sts along the selvedge edge of the hem, then K the 20 sts held after binding off the side seam, then pickup and K 10 sts along the selvedge edge of the other hem, ending at the bottom corner. 40 sts on needle.

Row 1 (WS): Knit.

Row 2 (RS): K17, Sssk, K3tog, K17. 36 sts.

Row 3: Knit.

BO sts Kwise.

Repeat for the other side.

Cuffs

Begin in the middle of the cuff edge of a side panel, at the seam created by the 3-Needle bind off. With RS facing, join C3 and PU and K 5 (6, 6, 6, 8, 8, 8, 10, 10) sts along the edge of the side panel, K the held sts, PU and K 6 (7, 7, 7, 9, 9, 9, 11, 11) sts along the remaining edge of the side panel, PM. 44 (52, 56, 62, 70, 74, 80, 88, 94) sts.

Work Corrugated Rib in the round for 2". Use C3 to BO.

Repeat for other Cuff.

Finishing

Weave in ends, wash and block to Schematic measurements.

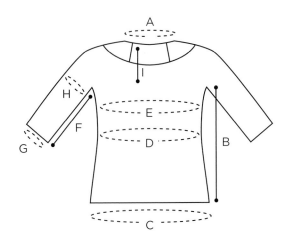

A 15.25 (16, 17.5, 19, 20..25, 21, 23.25, 24.75, 25.5)"
B 17 (17, 17, 17, 17, 18, 18, 18, 18)"
C 33.5 (36.25, 40.25, 44.25, 48.25, 52.25, 54, 58.75, 63)"
D 23.25 (26, 30, 34, 38.25, 42.5, 44, 47, 51)"
E 30 (34, 38, 42, 46.75, 50.25, 54.25, 58.25, 62.25)"
F 11 (12.5, 13.25, 14.25, 15, 15.5, 15.5, 15.75, 16)"
G 8 (9.5, 10.25, 11.25, 12.75, 13.5, 14.5, 16, 17)"
H 11.75 (13.75, 14.5, 16.25, 18.5, 19.5, 20.75, 22.5, 23.75)"
I 10 (10.75, 11.75, 12.25, 12.5, 13, 13.5, 14, 14.5)"

ROSALYN TUNIC

by Tabetha A. Hedrick

FINISHED MEASUREMENTS

31.75 (36.25, 40.25, 44.25, 48, 52.25, 56)" finished bust measurement; garment is meant to be worn with 1.75 - 2.25" of positive ease

YARN

Knit Picks CotLin DK (70% Tanguis Cotton, 30% Linen; 123 yards/50g): Cerise 24835, 7 (8, 10, 11, 12, 13, 15) balls

NEEDLES

US 6 (4mm) 24" circular needles and DPN's, or size to obtain gauge

NOTIONS

Yarn Needle
Stitch Markers (optional)
Locking Stitch Markers (4)
Cable Needle

GAUGE

27 sts and 31 rows = 4" over Rosalyn Pattern, lightly stretched and blocked

Rosalyn Tunic

Notes:

Featuring a light cable pattern, this tunic is worked flat and seamed. The stitch pattern is worked in the center of both pieces, bordered by Reverse St st (K on WS, P on RS).

When there aren't enough stitches to work a complete cable, just knit the stitches. When working the chart, follow RS rows (even numbers) from right to left, and WS rows (odd numbers) from left to right.

Rosalyn Stitch (multiples of 19 sts +10)

Rows 1, 3, 5 (WS): K2, P6, K2, *P9, K2, P6, K2; rep from * 5 (6, 6, 7, 8, 8, 9) times.

Row 2 (RS): *P2, 1/2 RC, 1/2 LC, P2, 1/3 LC, K1, 1/3 RC; rep from * 5 (6, 6, 7, 8, 8, 9) times, P2, 1/2 RC, 1/2 LC, P2.

Row 4: *P2, 1/2 RC, 1/2 LC, P2, K9; rep from * 5 (6, 6, 7, 8, 8, 9) times, P2, 1/2 RC, 1/2 LC, P2.

Rep Rows 2 - 5 for pattern.

1/2 LC: Slip 1 stitch to CN and hold in front; K2, K1 from CN.
1/2 RC: Slip 2 stitches to CN and hold in back; K1, K2 from CN.
1/3 LC: Slip 1 stitch to CN and hold in front; K3, K1 from CN.
1/3 RC: Slip 3 stitches to CN and hold in back; K1, K3 from CN.

DIRECTIONS

Back

CO 115 (126, 140, 153, 166, 180, 193) sts.

Row 1 (WS): K5 (1, 8, 5, 2, 9, 6), PM, work Row 1 of Rosalyn Stitch, PM, K5 (1, 8, 5, 2, 9, 6).

Row 2 (RS): K1, P to marker, work next row of Rosalyn Stitch to marker, P to last st, K1.

Row 3: K to marker, work next row of Rosalyn Stitch to marker, K to end.

Rep Rows 2 and 3 two more times.

Shape Waist

Note: The decreases for the waist shaping should be worked depending on what the next stitch in the pattern is supposed to be: for purl stitches, use a p2tog-tbl at the beginning of the row and a p2tog at the end of the row; for knit stitch, use an ssk at the beginning of the row and a k2tog at the end of the row.

*Dec Row (RS): K1, dec 1 st, work in pat as established to last 3 sts, dec 1 st, K1. 2 sts dec.

Work 15 rows even in established pat. Rep from * 0 (1, 0, 2, 2, 2, 2) more times. 113 (122, 138, 147, 160, 174, 187) sts.

Sizes 31.75 (36.25, 40.25) ONLY:

*Rep Dec Row. Work 17 rows even in established pat. Rep from * 1 (0, 1) time(s). 109 (120, 134) sts rem.

All Sizes:

Work even in established pat until back measures a finished length of 8.75 (8.5, 8.75, 8.25, 8.25, 8.25, 8.25)″ from CO edge, ending with a WS row.

Note: The increases for waist shaping should be worked dependent on what the next stitch in the pattern is supposed to be: for purl stitches, use a M1P and for knit stitches, use a M1.

Size 31.75 ONLY: Work 54 rows even in established pat.

Sizes 36.25 (40.25, 44.25, 48, 52.25, 56) ONLY:

*Inc Row (RS): K1, inc 1 st, work in pat as established to last st, inc 1 st, K1. 2 sts inc.

Work 27 (27, 32, 33, 34, 36) rows even in established pat. Rep from * 1 (0, 0, 1, 0, 0) times. 124 (136, 149, 164, 176, 189) sts.

Sizes 40.25 (44.25, 52.25, 56) ONLY:

Inc Row (RS): K1, inc 1 st, work in pat as established to last 1 st, K1. 2 sts inc. Work 29 (33, 35, 37) rows even in established pat. 138 (151, 178, 191) sts.

All sizes, final stitch counts: 109 (124, 138, 151, 164, 178, 191) sts.

All Sizes:

Place locking stitch marker into the first and last stitch of last row worked.

Work even in established pat until back measures 6.75 (7.25, 7.5, 8, 8.25, 8.25, 9)″ from marker placement. Do not remove markers.

Shape Shoulders

BO 6 (8, 8, 10, 10, 10, 12) sts at beg of next 4 rows, then 7 (5, 8, 7, 9, 11, 9) sts at beg of next 2 rows. BO rem 71 (82, 90, 97, 106, 116, 125) sts.

Front

CO 115 (126, 140, 153, 166, 180, 193) sts.

Row 1 (WS): K5 (1, 8, 5, 2, 9, 6), PM, work Row 1 of Rosalyn Stitch, PM, K5 (1, 8, 5, 2, 9, 6).

Row 2 (RS): K1, P to marker, work next row of Rosalyn Stitch to marker, P to last st, K1.

Row 3: K to marker, work next row of Rosalyn Stitch to marker, K to end.

Rep Rows 2 and 3 two more times.

Shape Waist

Note: The decreases for the waist shaping should be worked depending on what the next stitch in the pattern is supposed to be: for purl stitches, use a p2tog-tbl at the beginning of the row and a p2tog at the end of the row; for knit stitch, use an ssk at the beginning of the row and a k2tog at the end of the row.

*Dec Row (RS): K1, dec 1 st, work in pat as established to last 3 sts, dec 1 st, K1. 2 sts dec.

Work 15 rows even in established pat. Rep from * 0 (1, 0, 2, 2, 2, 2) more times. 113 (122, 138, 147, 160, 174, 187) sts.

Sizes 31.75 (36.25, 40.25) ONLY:

*Rep Dec Row. Work 17 rows even in established pat. Rep from * 1 (0, 1) time(s). 109 (120, 134) sts rem.

All Sizes:

Work even in established pat until front measures a finished length of 8.75 (8.5, 8.75, 8.25, 8.25, 8.25, 8.25)″ from CO edge, ending with a WS row.

Note: The increases for waist shaping should be worked dependent on what the next stitch in the pattern is supposed to be: for purl stitches, use a M1P and for knit stitches, use a M1.

Size 31.75 ONLY: Work 54 rows even in established pat.

Sizes 36.25 (40.25, 44.25, 48, 52.25, 56) ONLY:

*Inc Row (RS): K1, inc 1 st, work in pat as established to last st, inc 1 st, K1. 2 sts inc. Work 27 (27, 32, 33, 34, 36) rows even in established pat. Rep from * 1 (0, 0, 1, 0, 0) times. 124 (136, 149, 164, 176, 189) sts.

Sizes 40.25 (44.25, 52.25, 56) ONLY:

Inc Row (RS): K1, inc 1 st, work in pat as established to last st, inc 1 st, K1. 2 sts inc. Work 29 (33, 35, 37) rows even in established pat. 138 (151, 178, 191) sts.

All sizes, final stitch counts: 109 (124, 138, 151, 164, 178, 191) sts.

All Sizes:

Place locking stitch marker into the first and last stitch of last row worked.

Work even in established pat until front measures 5.5 (6, 5.75, 6.25, 6, 6.25, 6.5)″ from marker placement. Do not remove markers.

Shape Front Neck

Work 36 (41, 48, 51, 55, 60, 64) sts, join 2nd ball of yarn and BO center 37 (42, 42, 49, 54, 58, 63) sts, work to end of row. Working both sides AT THE SAME TIME with separate balls of yarn, work 1 WS row even.

Note: Use the sloped BO for a smooth neck edge.

Row 1 (RS): Work even in pat to neck edge, move to other side of neck, BO 4 (5, 4, 4, 3, 3, 3) st(s) at beg of neck, continue in pat to end of row.

Row 2 (WS): Work even in pat to neck edge, move to other side of neck, BO 4 (5, 4, 4, 3, 3, 3) sts at beg of neck, continue in pat to end of row.

Repeat last 2 rows 2 (3, 5, 5, 5, 6, 4) more times. 24 (21, 24, 27, 37, 39, 49) sts rem on each side.

Sizes 31.75 (48, 52.25, 56) ONLY:

Row 1 (RS): Work even in pat to neck edge, move to other side of neck, BO 5 (4, 4, 4) st(s) at beg of neck, work in pat to end of row.

Row 2 (WS): Work even in pat to neck edge, move to other side of neck, BO 5 (4, 4, 4) sts at beg of neck, cont in pat to end of row.

Repeat Rows last 2 rows 0 (1, 1, 3) more times. 19 (29, 31, 33) sts rem on each side.

All Sizes
Shape Shoulders

BO 6 (8, 8, 10, 10, 10, 12) sts at beg of next 4 rows, then the rem 7 (5, 8, 7, 9, 11, 9) sts at beg of next 2 rows.

Finishing

Weave in ends, wash and block to diagram. Note that the circumferences shown include selvedge sts, the seamed Tunic will measure 0.5″ less around.
Sew shoulder seams. Sew side seams from hem to stitch marker placement on each side.

Neckband: With 24″ circular needle and RS facing, beg at right shoulder seam and pick up and knit 1 sts for every bound off st and 3 sts for every 4 rows around neckline. Join to work in the round. Purl 1 rnd. BO loosely.

Armbands: With DPN's and RS facing, beg at armhole seam and pick up and knit 1 sts for every bound off st and 3 sts for every 4 rows around armhole. Join to work in the round. Purl 1 rnd. BO loosely.

Weave in any remaining ends.

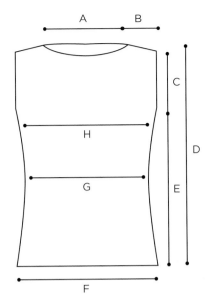

A 10.5 (12.4, 13.25, 14.25, 15.75, 17.25, 18.5)″
B 2.75 (3, 3.5, 4, 4.25, 4.5, 5)″
C 6.75 (7.25, 7.5, 8, 8.25, 8.75, 9)″
D 23.25 (23.75, 24.5, 25.5, 26, 26.75, 27.5)″
E 15.75 (15.75, 16.25, 16.75, 17, 17.25, 17.75)″
F 17 (18.75, 20.75, 22.75, 24.5, 26.75, 28.5)″
G 16.25 (17.75, 19.75, 21.75, 23.75, 25.75, 27.75)″
H 16.25 (18.25, 20.5, 22.25, 24.25, 26.25, 28.25)″

Rosalyn Stitch Chart

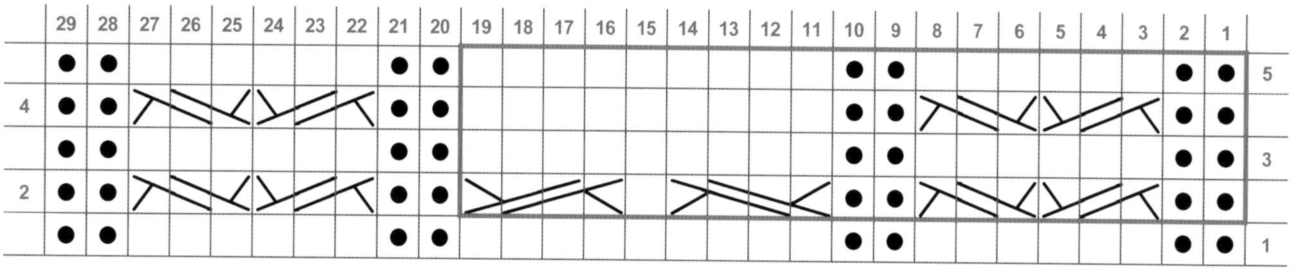
29 28 27 26 25 24 23 22 21 20 19 18 17 16 15 14 13 12 11 10 9 8 7 6 5 4 3 2 1
5
4
3
2
1

Legend

purl
RS: purl stitch
WS: knit stitch

knit
RS: knit stitch
WS: purl stitch

1/2 RC
sl2 to CN, hold in back. k1, k2 from CN

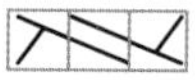

1/2 LC
sl 1 to CN, hold in front. k2, k1 from CN

1/3 LC
RS: sl1 to CN, hold in front. k3, k1 from CN

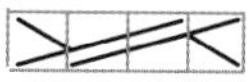

1/3 RC
RS: sl3 st to CN, hold in back. k1, k3 from CN

pattern repeat

HYPERION PULLOVER

by Laura Birek

For pattern support, contact info@laurabirek.com

FINISHED MEASUREMENTS

28 (32, 36, 40, 44, 48, 52, 56, 60)" finished bust measurement; garment is meant to be worn with 0" of ease

YARN

Knit Picks Comfy Fingering (75% Pima Cotton, 25% Acrylic; 218 yards/50g): Blackberry 24824, 4 (4, 5, 6, 6, 7, 7, 8, 8) balls

NEEDLES

US 3 (3.25mm) straight or circular needles, or size to obtain Sleeve/Yoke gauge
US 5 (3.75mm) 24" circular needles (or longer for sizes 40" and above), or size to obtain Body gauge

NOTIONS

Yarn Needle
Stitch Markers
Split-ring Markers or Safety Pins
Scrap Yarn or Stitch Holder
Size F Crochet Hook (optional)

GAUGE

28 sts and 32 rows = 4" with smaller needles over Honeycomb Lace Stitch, blocked, for Sleeves/Yoke
24 sts and 32 rows = 4" with smaller needles in St st, blocked, for Sleeves/Yoke. (Because gauge is difficult to measure in the Honeycomb Stitch, a St st gauge is included for reference)
22 sts and 28 rows = 4" with larger needles in St st worked in the round, blocked, for Body

Hyperion Pullover

Notes:

The top of this pattern is knit flat from cuff to cuff, with a split in the middle for the neck opening. Then the arms are seamed, and then the body is picked up and worked in the round.

If using the chart, RS rows (odd numbers) are read from right to left, and WS rows (even numbers) from left to right.

Purl Into the Front and Knit Into the Back (PFKB)

When you work the Honeycomb Lace stitch, every time you come to a double-wrapped yo on a wrong side, you will do this stitch. It's a slight variation on PFB (purl into the front and back of a st). P into the first yo, drop only one loop from the yo off your left needle, then move your yarn to the back and K through the remaining loop on the yo. 2 sts.

Honeycomb Lace Stitch (worked flat over multiples of 4 sts plus 6 sts)

Row 1: SL1, K1, K2tog, *yo twice, SKP, K2tog*, rep from * to * until last 2 sts, yo, K2.
Row 2: SL1, P2, *P2, PFKB*, rep from * to * until last 3 sts, P3.
Row 3: SL1, K1, yo, *SKP, K2tog, yo twice*, rep from * to * until last 4 sts, SKP, K2.
Row 4: SL1, P2, *PFKB, P2*, rep from * to * until last 3 sts, P3.

DIRECTIONS
Sleeves and Yoke

The sleeves are worked flat from the cuff to cuff. At the neck opening, you will place half the sts on a holder and work each side independently before joining to finish the other sleeve.

Left Sleeve

With smaller needle, loosely CO 66 (74, 82, 94, 102, 110, 118, 126, 134) sts. P one row, then begin working Honeycomb Lace Stitch Row 1, from either the chart or line-by-line instructions.
Work even in Honeycomb Lace Stitch until sleeve measures 7 (7.5, 8, 8.5, 9, 9.5, 10, 10, 10)" from CO edge. Place one split-ring marker or safety pin on both edges of work – this will mark where your underarm seam ends.

Continue working even in Honeycomb Lace Stitch for another 5.5 (5.5, 6, 6, 6.5, 6.5, 7, 6.5, 6.5)" until your piece measures 12.5 (13, 14, 14.5, 15.5, 16, 17, 16.5, 16.5)" from CO edge, ending on Row 3 of stitch pat.

Split for Neck Opening

Work first 30 (34, 38, 46, 50, 54, 58, 62, 66) sts in Row 4 of stitch pat, BO 6 (6, 6, 2, 2, 2, 2, 2, 2) sts, place the just-worked sts onto holder, continue working remaining 30 (34, 38, 46, 50, 54, 58, 62, 66) sts in pat.
Turn work. You will now work each side separately, starting with the back side. Be careful to keep 3 selvedge stitches at the edges of your work. For the neck split, you will work the Honeycomb Lace Stitch as follows:
Row 1: SL1, K1, K2tog, *yo twice, SKP, K2tog*, rep from * to * 6 (7, 8, 10, 11, 12, 13, 14, 15) times, yo, K2.
Row 2: SL1, P2, *P2, PFKB*, rep from * to * 6 (7, 8, 10, 11, 12, 13, 14, 15) times, P3.
Row 3: SL1, K1, yo, *SKP, K2tog, yo twice*, rep from * to * 6 (7, 8,

10, 11, 12, 13, 14, 15) times, SKP, K2.
Row 4: SL1, P2, *PFKB, P2*, rep from * to * 6 (7, 8, 10, 11, 12, 13, 14, 15) times, P3.

Work back side of yoke even in Honeycomb Lace Stitch for 10 (11, 12, 13, 14, 14, 15, 15, 16)" ending with Row 4 of stitch pat. Leave ball of yarn attached and place stitches on holder while you finish the front side of the yoke.

Place front yoke sts onto needles, and with new ball of yarn, begin working from Row 1 of stitch pat the same as for the back side of the yoke. Work even for 10 (11, 12, 13, 14, 14, 15, 15, 16)" in Honeycomb Lace, ending with Row 4 of stitch pat.

Break yarn, and, being careful not to twist the work, place 30 (34, 38, 46, 50, 54, 58, 62, 66) sts from holder onto needle.

Right Arm

You now have two separated sets of sts on one needle. You should be on a Row 1, and will knit to the gap, then CO sts and continue knitting to join the sts together as one. I recommend using a knitted cast-on, as this will be more stable as a neckline.

SL1, K1, K2tog, *yo twice, SKP, K2tog*, rep from * to * 6 (7, 8, 10, 11, 12, 13, 14, 15) times, yo, K2, CO 6 (6, 6, 2, 2, 2, 2, 2, 2) sts, K2, K2tog, *yo twice, SKP, K2tog*, rep from * to * 6 (7, 8, 10, 11, 12, 13, 14, 15) times, yo, K2. 66 (74, 82, 94, 102, 110, 118, 126, 134) sts

Continue working even in Honeycomb Lace Stitch for 5.5 (5.5, 6, 6, 6.5, 6.5, 7, 6.5, 6.5)". Place split ring markers on each edge of work to mark where your armhole seam will end.

Continue working in Honeycomb Lace Stitch until sleeve measures 7 (7.5, 8, 8.5, 9, 9.5, 10, 10, 10)" from markers, or 35 (37, 40, 42, 45, 46, 49, 48, 49)" from CO edge, ending with a RS row. P one row, without slipping first st.
BO loosely.

Seam Arms

Block yoke to schematic lengths. With yarn needle, use mattress stitch to seam the left arm from cuff to the split-ring marker. Repeat on right side. Leave yarn ends loose until the garment is completed.

Body
Bust

With larger needle, PU 77 (88, 99, 110, 121, 132, 143, 154, 165) sts evenly from underarm to underarm on back side of garment, place marker, PU 77 (88, 99, 110, 121, 132, 143, 154, 165) sts evenly on front side of garment, place marker and begin working in the round. 154 (176, 198, 220, 242, 264, 286, 308, 330) sts total.
Work even in St st (K every round) for 4.75 (4.75, 4.75, 4.25, 4, 3.5, 3.25, 3, 2.5)"

Waist Decreases

Waist decreases are worked in 4-round repeats.
Decrease Round: *K1, K2tog, K to last 3 sts before marker, SKP, K1, SM, repeat from * once more. 4 sts dec. 150 (172, 194, 216, 238, 260, 282, 304, 326) sts.
K 3 rounds even.
Repeat above 4 rounds 10 times more. 110 (132, 154, 176, 198, 220, 242, 264, 286) sts.

Waist Increases

Waist increases are also worked in 4-round repeats.

Increase Round: *K1, m1L, K to last st before marker, m1R, K1, SM, repeat from * once more. 4 sts inc. 114 (136, 158, 180, 202, 224, 246, 268, 290) sts.

K 3 rounds even.

Repeat above 4 rounds 7 (7, 8, 8, 8, 8, 9, 9, 9) times more. 142 (164, 190, 212, 234, 256, 282, 304, 326) sts.

Hem

Next 4 Rounds: *K2, P2, rep from * to end of round.
BO loosely in rib.

Honeycomb Lace Chart

	10	9	8	7	6	5	4	3	2	1	
4	V			●	—						
			\	O	O	/	\	O		V		3
2	V					●	—				
			O	/	\	O	O	/		V		1

Legend

| V | **slip**
RS: Slip stitch as if to purl, holding yarn in back
WS: Slip stitch as if to purl, holding yarn in front |

| ☐ | **knit**
RS: knit stitch
WS: purl stitch |

| / | **k2tog**
RS: Knit two stitches together as one stitch
WS: Purl 2 stitches together |

| O | **yo**
yarn over |

| \ | **ssk**
RS: Sl 1 st kwise, sl another st kwise. Insert left-hand needle into front of these 2 sts and k tog

WS: P 2 sts tog in back loops, inserting needle from left, behind and into the backs of the 2nd & 1st sts in that order |

| ● — | **purl into front, knit into back**
WS: P into the first YO, drop only one loop from the YO off left needle, then move yarn to the back and K through the remaining loop on the YO. |

Finishing

If you'd like to reinforce the neckline, with a crochet hook work single crochet around entire neck hole opening. Be careful to check for puckering or rippling of the fabric, you may need to try a number of different hook sizes to match your gauge.

Weave in ends, using loose ends to reinforce underarm if needed. Wash and block to diagram.

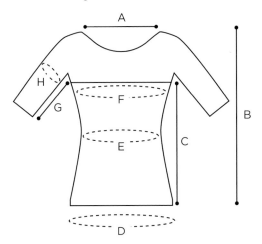

A 10 (11, 12, 13, 14, 14, 15, 15, 16)"
B 21 (21.5, 22.5, 23, 23.25, 23.25, 24, 24.5, 24.5)"
C 16.25 (16.25, 16.75, 16.25, 16, 15.5, 15.75, 15.5, 15)"
D 25.75 (29.75, 34.5, 38.5, 42.5, 46.5, 51.25, 55.25, 59.25)"
E 20 (24, 28, 32, 36, 40, 44, 48, 52)"
F 28 (32, 36, 40, 44, 48, 52, 56, 60)"
G 7 (7.5, 8, 8.5, 9, 9.5, 10, 10, 10)"
H 9.25 (10.25, 11.5, 13.25, 14.25, 15.5, 16.5, 17.75, 18.75)"

ELVA CARDIGAN

by Triona Murphy

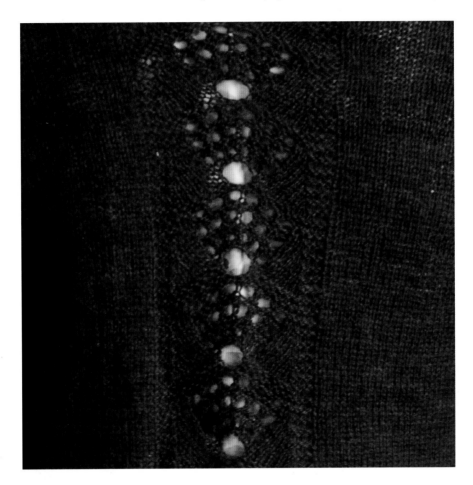

FINISHED MEASUREMENTS

29 (32, 36, 40, 44, 48, 52, 56)" finished bust measurement; garment is meant to be worn with 0-2" of positive ease

YARN

Knit Picks Shadow (100% Merino; 440 yards/50g): Nocturne Heather 24842, 2 (3, 3, 3, 4, 4, 4, 4) hanks

NEEDLES

US 4 (3.5mm) 24-40" circular needles and DPNs or two 24" circular needles for two circulars technique, or one 32" or longer circular needle for Magic Loop technique, or 2 sizes smaller than needle to obtain gauge. US 6 (4.0mm) 24-40" circular needles and DPNs or two 24" circular needles for two

circulars technique, or one 32" or longer circular needle for Magic Loop technique, or size to obtain gauge

NOTIONS

Yarn Needle
Stitch Markers
Waste Yarn
Spare DPNs or circular needle, of gauge size or smaller

GAUGE

24 sts and 32 rows = 4" with larger needles in St st, blocked.
20 sts and 32 rows = 4" with larger needles in Garter Fan Pattern, blocked

Elva Cardigan

Notes:

This flowy, lightweight cardigan is designed to be worn open or with a skinny belt. Constructed from the bottom up, the sweater is worked seamlessly with raglan sleeve shaping. The elbow-length sleeves are worked with a slight flare at the cuff and then joined to the body at the yoke.

Length measurements for the sleeves and body on the schematic are taken with the edges rolled, so they may be shorter than what is written in the pattern.

The Garter Fan Pattern can be worked from either the chart or line-by-line directions, below. If working from the chart, read RS (even numbered) rows from right to left, and WS (odd numbered) rows from left to right.

Garter Fan Pattern for sizes 29, 32, 36, 40" (worked flat over 20 sts)

Row 1 (WS): K all sts.
Row 2 (RS): K all sts.
Row 3: K all sts.
Row 4: K10, yo twice (double yo), K10. 22 sts.
Row 5: K3, P7, m5 sts in one (drop first loop of double yo from previous row, K1, P1, K1, P1, K1 into elongated stitch), P7, K3. 25 sts.
Row 6: K2, ssk, K17, K2tog, K2. 23 sts.
Row 7: K3, P17, K3.
Row 8: K2, ssk, K5, *yo, K1* six times, K4, K2tog, K2. 27 sts.
Row 9: K3, P5, K11, P5, K3.
Row 10: K2, ssk, K19, K2tog, K2. 25 sts.
Row 11: K3, P4, K11, P4, K3.
Row 12: K2, ssk, K2, *ssk, yo* three times, K1, *yo, K2tog* three times, K2, K2tog, K2. 23 sts.
Row 13: K3, P3, K11, P3, K3.
Row 14: K2, ssk, K15, K2tog, K2. 21 sts.
Row 15: K3, P2, K11, P2, K3.
Row 16: K2, ssk twice, *yo, ssk* twice, yo, K1, *yo, K2tog* three times, K4. 20 sts.
Repeat Rows 1-16 for Garter Fan Pattern.

Garter Fan Pattern for sizes 44, 48, 52, 56" (worked flat over 28 sts)

Row 1 (WS): K all sts.
Row 2 (RS): K all sts.
Row 3: K all sts.
Row 4: K14, yo twice (double yo), K14. 30 sts.
Row 5: K5, P9, (drop first loop of double yo from previous row, K1, P1, K1, P1, K1 into elongated stitch), P9, K5. 33 sts.
Row 6: K4, ssk, K21, K2tog, K4. 31 sts.
Row 7: K5, P21, K5.
Row 8: K4, ssk, K6, *yo, K1* eight times, K5, K2tog, K4. 37 sts.
Row 9: K5, P6, K15, P6, K5.
Row 10: K4, ssk, K25, K2tog, K4. 35 sts.
Row 11: K5, P5, K15, P5, K5.
Row 12: K4, ssk, K3, *ssk, yo* four times, K1, *yo, K2tog* four times, K3, K2tog, K4. 33 sts.
Row 13: K5, P4, K15, P4, K5.
Row 14: K4, ssk, K21, K2tog, K4. 31 sts.

Row 15: K5, P3, K15, P3, K5.
Row 16: K3, ssk three times, *yo, ssk* three times, yo, K1, *yo, K2tog* four times, K2tog, K5. 28 sts.
Repeat Rows 1-16 for Garter Fan Pattern.

Kitchener Stitch (grafting)

With an equal number of sts on two needles, break yarn leaving several feet of tail and thread through yarn needle. Hold needles parallel, with WS's facing in and both needles pointing to the right. Perform Step 2 on the first front st, and then Step 4 on the first back st, and then continue with instructions below.

1: Pull yarn needle kwise through front st and drop st from knitting needle.
2: Pull yarn needle pwise through next front st, leave st on knitting needle.
3: Pull yarn needle pwise through first back st and drop st from knitting needle.
4: Pull yarn needle kwise through next back st, leave st on knitting needle.
Repeat steps 1 – 4 until all sts have been grafted.

DIRECTIONS
Lower Body

Using smaller 24-40" circular needle, CO 168 (184, 208, 232, 256, 280, 304, 328) sts. Do not join. Working back and forth in rows, work 6 rows in St st (K on RS, P on WS), ending with a WS row.

Switch to larger 24-40" circular needle and work setup row.
Setup Row (RS): K39 (43, 49, 55, 61, 67, 73, 79) sts, PM for side, K35 (39, 45, 51, 53, 59, 65, 71) sts, PM for motif, K20 (20, 20, 20, 28, 28, 28, 28) sts, PM for motif, K35 (39, 45, 51, 53, 59, 65, 71) sts, PM for other side, K39 (43, 49, 55, 61, 67, 73, 79) sts to end.
Next Row (WS): Purl to motif marker, work Row 1 of the correct Garter Fan Pattern for your size (using written instructions or chart) over next 20 (20, 20, 20, 28, 28, 28, 28) sts, purl to end.

Continue in St st, working Garter Fan Pattern between the two central markers, until work measures 10" from CO edge (flatten curling edge down when measuring), ending with a WS row.

Begin waist shaping.
Waist Decrease Row (RS): [Knit to 6 sts from first side marker, K2tog, K4, slip marker, K4, ssk] twice, working Garter Fan Pattern between motif markers as established. Knit to end of row. 4 sts dec.
Repeat Waist Decrease Row every 10th (8th, 10th, 8th, 10th, 10th, 8th, 8th) row, two more times. 12 sts dec total, 156 (172, 196, 220, 244, 268, 292, 316) sts.

Work even in pattern as set until work measures 14.75 (14, 13.75, 13.5, 14.75, 14.25, 13.75, 12.5)" from CO edge (flatten curling edge down when measuring), ending with a WS row.

Begin neck shaping.
Note: Neck decreases will continue past the sleeve join and through the yoke section. Read ahead through the rest of the lower body section.
Neck Decrease Row (RS): K1, ssk, work in pattern to 3 sts from end of row, K2tog, K1. 2 sts decreased.
Repeat Neck Decrease Row every 12th (10th, 10th, 8th, 6th, 4th, 4th, 4th) row, 3 (4, 8, 11, 14, 16, 19, 23) more times.

When you've completed 7 full repeats of the Garter Fan Pattern, as well as 13 (7, 5, 3, 13, 9, 5, 3) rows of the next repeat, set work aside. Do not cut yarn. Use a separate ball to work the sleeves.

Sleeves (make 2)

Using smaller DPNs or preferred needle for working sleeves in the round, CO 60 (66, 70, 78, 84, 94, 100, 106) sts. Join for working in the round, being careful not to twist. PM to mark the beginning of the round.

Work 6 rnds in St st.

Switch to larger needles and work 1″ even in St st, then begin cuff decreases.

Cuff Decrease Rnd: K1, K2tog, knit to 3 sts from end, ssk, K1. 2 sts dec.

Work Cuff Decrease Rnd every other rnd, two more times. 54 (60, 64, 72, 78, 88, 94, 100) sts.

Work 1″ even in St st, then begin sleeve increases.

Sleeve Increase Rnd: K1, M1L, knit to 1 st from end, M1R, K1. 2 sts inc.

Repeat Sleeve Increase Rnd every 13th (13th, 11th, 12th, 12th, 13th, 13th, 13th) rnd, 4 (4, 5, 5, 5, 5, 5, 5) more times. 64 (70, 76, 84, 90, 100, 106, 112) sts.

Work sleeve even until work measures 12.5 (12.5, 13, 13.5, 13.5, 14, 14, 14)″ from CO edge (flatten curling edge down when measuring).

Next Rnd: Remove beginning of rnd marker, K4 (4, 5, 6, 6, 7, 7, 8) sts, slip last 8 (8, 10, 12, 12, 14, 14, 16) sts worked to waste yarn. Do not bind off. Cut yarn, leaving a tail of at least 12″.

If it's the first sleeve you've worked, slip live sts to a spare set of DPNs or a spare circular needle before working the second sleeve. Leave working needles in the second sleeve when finished.

Yoke

Joining Row (RS): With yarn and needles still attached to Lower Body, knit to 4 (4, 5, 6, 6, 7, 7, 8) sts before first side marker, PM for raglan decreases, slip next 8 (8, 10, 12, 12, 14, 14, 16) sts to waste yarn (remove side marker when you come to it). Knit across all sts of first sleeve, PM for raglan decreases, work in pattern as set, including the next row of Garter Fan Pattern, to 4 (4, 5, 6, 6, 7, 7, 8) sts before second side marker, PM for raglan decreases, slip next 8 (8, 10, 12, 12, 14, 14, 16) sts to waste yarn (removing side marker). Knit across all sts of second sleeve, PM for raglan decreases, knit to end.

You should have 56 (62, 66, 72, 78, 86, 92, 96) sts for each sleeve. (Front and back sts will vary, depending on where you are on the neck shaping and the Garter Fan Pattern.)

Next Row (WS): Work even in pattern as established (work next row of Garter Fan Pattern between motif markers, purl all other sts).

Begin raglan decreases.

Raglan Decrease Row 1 (RS): [Work in pattern to 2 sts from raglan marker, ssk, slip marker, K2tog] four times, work in pattern to end. 8 sts decreased.

Raglan Decrease Row 2 (WS): [Work in pattern to 2 sts from raglan marker, P2tog, slip marker, P2togtbl] four times, work in pattern to end. 8 sts decreased.

While maintaining pattern as established (including neck decreases as given in Lower Body section), repeat both Raglan Decrease Rows 0 (0, 0, 1, 1, 2, 3, 3) more times.

Now work Raglan Decrease Row 1 on RS rows only (maintaining pattern on WS rows) 24 (27, 28, 28, 31, 32, 33, 34) more times.

When all Raglan and Neck Decrease Rows have been worked, you should have just completed Row 16 of the Garter Fan Pattern. You should have 36 (38, 50, 60, 66, 74, 80, 92) sts on the needles, divided as follows:

2 sts for each front, 4 (4, 6, 8, 8, 10, 10, 12) sts for each sleeve, 24 (26, 34, 40, 46, 50, 56, 64) sts for the back.

Work one WS row even (knit all sts between motif markers), then BO all sts loosely.

Finishing

Graft Underarms

Place held sts from body on one larger DPN. Place held sts from sleeve on another larger DPN. Graft (Kitchener stitch) sts together. Use the tails and/or short lengths of the working yarn to sew up any holes at the edges.

Front Bands

Using smaller 24-40″ circular needle, beginning at lower right-hand corner of sweater with the RS facing, pick up and knit 3 sts for every 4 rows along the right front edge, 1 st for every BO st along the back neck, and 3 sts for every 4 rows down the left front edge. The exact number of sts you pick up doesn't matter, but make sure it's an odd number.

Begin 1x1 rib:

Row 1 (WS): *P1, K1, rep from * to last st, P1.

Row 2 (RS): *K1, P1, rep from * to last st, K1.

Repeat Rows 1 and 2 until band measures 1″, then work Row 1 once more.

Work 4 rows in St st, then BO all sts loosely (you may want to use a needle a size or two bigger than the working needle for the BO).

Finishing

Weave in ends, wash, and block to diagram.

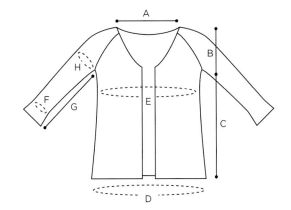

A 4 (4.25, 5.75, 6.75, 7.75, 8.25, 9.25, 10.75)″
B 6.5 (7.25, 7.5, 7.75, 8.5, 9, 9.5, 9.75)″
C 15.75 (15, 14.75, 14.5, 15.75, 15.25, 14.75, 14.5)″
D 28.25 (31, 35, 39, 43.25, 47.25, 51.25, 55.25)″
E 26.25 (29, 33, 37, 41.25, 45.25, 49.25, 53.25)″
F 9 (10, 10.75, 12, 13, 14.75, 15.75, 16.75)″
G 11.5 (11.5, 12, 12.5, 12.5, 13, 13, 13)″
H 10.75 (11.75, 12.75, 14, 15, 16.75, 17.75, 18.75)″

Garter Fan Chart sizes 29-40

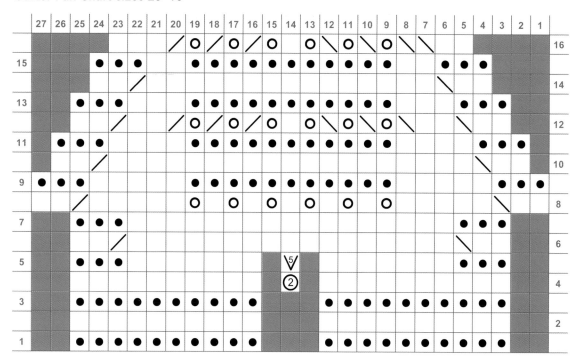

Legend

▨	**no stitch** placeholder - No stitch made.	⛛₅	**m5 sts in one** drop first loop of double YO from previous row, K1, P1, K1, P1, K1 into elongated stitch
●	**purl** RS: purl stitch WS: knit stitch	⧄	**k2tog** RS: Knit two stitches together as one stitch
☐	**knit** RS: knit stitch WS: purl stitch	O	**yo** yarn over
②	**yo twice** yarn over two times	⧅	**ssk** slip one stitch as if to knit, slip another stitch as if to knit. Insert left-hand needle into front of these 2 stitches and knit them together

Garter Fan Chart sizes 44-56

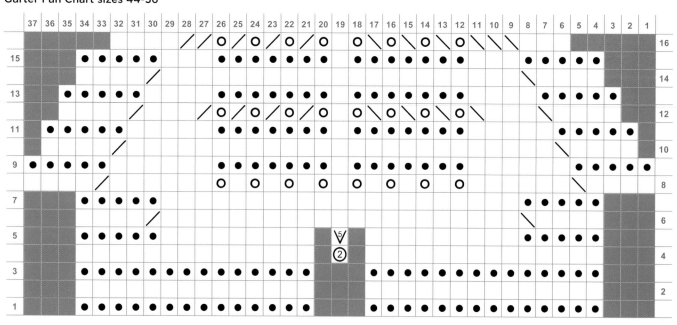

MARLIN

by Kristen Singer

FINISHED MEASUREMENTS

30.5 (34, 37.5, 42, 45.5, 50, 53.5, 58, 61.5, 66)″ finished bust measurement; garment is meant to be worn with positive ease

YARN

Knit Picks Shine Sport (60% Pima Cotton, 40% Modal® natural beech wood fiber; 110 yards/50g): MC Pageant 25339, 5 (5, 6, 6, 7, 7, 8, 8, 9, 9) balls; CC Platinum 25338 , 6 (6, 7, 7, 8, 8, 9, 9, 10, 10) balls

NEEDLES

US 5 (3.75mm) DPN's or long circular for Magic Loop, plus 24″ or longer circular needles depending on garment size, or size to obtain gauge

NOTIONS

Yarn Needle 2 Stitch Markers, in two colors

GAUGE

18 sts and 28 rows = 4″ in Stockinette Stitch in the round, blocked

Marlin

Notes:

A relaxed pullover, Marlin's different striped sections add variety and panache. A sporty dropped hem is created by working the Front and Back Hems separately and flat, knitting back and forth. Once the pieces have reached the length called for in the pattern instructions, the Front and Back pieces are joined together to work the rest of the body in the round. A gentle dropped shoulder is picked up from the armholes and fitted sleeves are knitted from the top down.

References to Right and Left are as worn.

1 x 1 Rib (worked flat over an odd number of sts)
Row 1 (RS): *K1, P1; rep from * to last stitch, K1.
Row 2 (WS): *P1, K1; rep from * to last stitch, P1.
Repeat Rows 1 and 2 for pat.

DIRECTIONS
Back Hem

Using CC and circular needles, CO 69 (77, 85, 95, 103, 113, 121, 131, 139, 149) sts.
Work in 1 x 1 Rib pattern for 6 rows.

Stockinette Stitch (St st) (with 4 Selvage sts each side)
Row 1 (RS): *K1, P1, rep from * 2 times, K to last 4 sts, *P1, K1, rep from * 2 times.
Row 2 (WS): *P1, K1, rep from * 2 times, P to last 4 sts, *K1, P1, rep from * 2 times.
Rep Rows 1 & 2 as established until 20 rows have been worked, ending with Row 2.
Set Back Hem aside.

Front Hem

Work as for Back Hem, working only 10 rows in St st with Selvage, rather than 20.

Body

With RS of Front Hem facing you, join MC, using MC K across sts of Front Hem, PM (to indicate side seam), K across held 69 (77, 85, 95, 103, 113, 121, 131, 139, 149) sts of Back Hem, PM (using marker of different color to indicate beg of rnd), and join for working in the round. 138 (154, 170, 190, 206, 226, 242, 262, 278, 298) sts.

Note:

You have now joined the Back and Front pieces together and will be working the rest of the pullover in the round. This joining row was Round One of the Stripe Pattern.

Body Stripe Pattern
Rounds 1 – 20: Using MC, K.
Rounds 21 – 40: Using CC, K.
Work Rounds 1 – 40 a total of 2 times, then work Rounds 1 – 20 one time more.

Separate Front & Back for Armhole & Neck Shaping
RS: Using CC, K across 69 (77, 85, 95, 103, 113, 121, 131, 139, 149) sts for Front and place remaining sts on a holder for working the Back later.

Front Neck
Continuing to use CC for remainder of Front, P 1 WS row.

Neck Shaping
Next Row (RS): K 27 (31, 33, 37, 39, 43, 45, 49, 51, 55) left front sts, BO center 15 (15, 19, 21, 25, 27, 31, 33, 37, 39) stitches, K across rem 27 (31, 33, 37, 39, 43, 45, 49, 51, 55) sts of right front.

Right Front
Purl 1 WS row to BO sts, turn work.
Decrease Row (RS): K2, SKP, K to end.
Work a Decrease Row every 4 (4, 5, 4, 4, 4, 4, 4, 4, 4) rows a total of 5 (5, 5, 7, 7, 7, 9, 9, 9, 10) times. 22 (26, 28, 30, 32, 36, 36, 40, 42, 45) sts.
Work even in St st (K on RS, P on WS) until Right Front measures 6 (6.5, 7, 7.5, 8, 8.5, 9, 9.5, 10, 10.5)" from Front and Back separation point.
Bind off all sts.

Left Front
Attach yarn, ready to begin a WS row at the neckline.
Purl 1 WS row even.
Decrease Row (RS): K to last 4 sts, K2tog, K2.
Work a Decrease Row every 4 (5, 4, 4, 4, 4, 4, 4, 4, 4) rows 5 (5, 5, 7, 7, 7, 9, 9, 9, 10) times. 22 (26, 28, 30, 32, 36, 36, 40, 42, 45) sts.
Work even in St st until Left Front measures 6 (6.5, 7, 7.5, 8, 8.5, 9, 9.5, 10, 10.5)" from Front and Back separation point.
Bind off all sts.

Back Neck
Using CC for remainder of Back, purl one WS row.
Work even in St st until piece measures 5 (5.5, 6, 6.5, 7, 7.5, 8, 8.5, 9, 9.5)" from Front and Back separation point, ending with a WS row.

Neck Shaping
RS: K across 24 (28, 30, 32, 34, 38, 38, 42, 44, 47) right back sts, BO center 21 (21, 25, 31, 35, 37, 45, 47, 51, 55) sts, K across rem 24 (28, 30, 32, 34, 38, 38, 42, 44, 47) left back sts.

Left Back
Purl 1 WS row, to BO sts, turn.
Decrease Row (RS): K2, SKP, K to end.
Work a Decrease Row every RS row a total of two times. 22 (26, 28, 30, 32, 36, 36, 40, 42, 45) sts.
Bind off all sts.

Right Back
Attach yarn at neckline, ready to begin a WS row. Purl 1 WS row.
Decrease Row (RS): K to last 4 sts, K2tog, K2.
Work a Decrease Row every RS row a total of two times. 22 (26, 28, 30, 32, 36, 36, 40, 42, 45) sts.
Bind off all stitches.

Finishing
Seam together Shoulder seams to prepare for working sleeves.

Sleeves (make 2)
Using MC, PU and K 48 (52, 56, 60, 64, 68, 72, 76, 80, 84) sts evenly around armhole opening. PM and begin working in the round.

Work even in St st (K every round) until upper arm measures 5 (5.5, 6, 6.5, 7, 6.5, 6, 5.5, 9, 8.5)".

Sleeve Shaping

Note: Decreases and Striping Pattern occur at the same time, read through both sections before proceeding.

Decrease Round: K1, K2tog, K to last 3 sts, SKP, K1.
Work a Decrease Round every 10 (10, 10, 8, 8, 8, 8, 8, 6, 6) rounds 8 (9, 10, 11, 12, 13, 14, 15, 16, 17) times. 32 (34, 36, 38, 40, 42, 44, 46, 48, 50) sts remain for cuff.

AT SAME TIME, when sleeve measures 8" from armhole, begin working Sleeve Stripe Pattern:
Sleeve Stripe Pattern
Rounds 1 – 4: Using CC, K. Rounds 5 – 8: Using MC, K.
Rep Rnds 1-8 for pat.
Work Sleeve Stripe Pattern while continuing Sleeve Shaping as established, until Sleeve measures approximately 3" less than desired length to wrist, ending with Row 8, then continue rest of sleeve in CC.
Using CC, K 1 Round.

Cuff

All Rounds: *K1, P1; rep from * to end of round.
Repeat until cuff measures approximately 3".
Bind off all sts.

Neckband

Using CC and with RS of work facing you, starting at Right Shoulder Seam, PU and K 1 st for every two rows worked along Right Back Neck Shaping, PU and K 21 (21, 25, 31, 35, 37, 45, 47, 51, 55) from Back Neck bound off sts, 1 st for every two rows worked along Left Back Neck Shaping, 1 st for every two rows worked along Left Front Neck Shaping, 15 (15, 19, 21, 25, 27, 31, 33, 37, 39) from Front Neck bound off sts, 1 st for every two rows worked along Right Front Neck Shaping – making sure to pick up an even number of sts.

PM and join for working in the round.
All Rnds: *K1, P1; rep from * to end of round.
Repeat for 6 rows.
Bind off all sts.

Finishing

Weave in ends, wash and block to diagram.

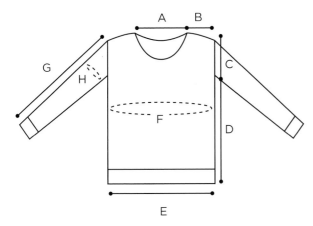

A 4 (4, 5, 5, 6, 6, 7, 7)"
B 4.5, (5.5, 6, 6.5, 7, 8, 8, 9)"
C 5 (5.5, 6, 6.5, 7, 7.5, 8, 8.5)"
D 15" (all sizes)
E 15 (17, 19, 21, 23, 25, 27, 29)"
F 30 (34, 42, 50, 58, 66, 74)"
G 21 (21.5, 22, 22.5, 23, 23.5, 24, 24.5)"
H 10 (11, 12, 13, 14, 15, 16, 17)"

RIVER WALK PULLOVER

by Erica Jackofsky

FINISHED MEASUREMENTS

32 (36.25, 40, 44.25, 48, 52.25, 56, 60.25, 64)" finished bust measurement; garment is meant to be worn with 1-2" of positive ease

YARN

Knit Picks Comfy Fingering (75% Pima Cotton, 25% Acrylic; 218 yards/50g): White 24812, 4 (5, 5, 6, 7, 7, 8, 9, 9) balls

NEEDLES

US 1.5 (2.5mm) 24-32" circular needle, or size to obtain gauge
US 1.5 (2.5mm) DPNs, Two 24" circular

needles for two circulars technique, or one 32" or longer circular needle for Magic Loop technique, or size to obtain gauge

NOTIONS

Yarn Needle
Stitch Markers
Scrap Yarn or Stitch Holder

GAUGE

30 sts and 38 rnds = 4" in stockinette st worked in the round, blocked
33 rounds = 4.5" in River Stitch pattern worked in the round, blocked

River Walk Pullover

Notes:

This short-sleeved tee uses dropped stitches to create a light and airy feel that's perfect for spring. If any change needs to be made in length to achieve a custom fit make sure that all increases and decreases fall on a plain knit round (Rounds 1-8 of the River Stitch pattern). Because the elongated stitches add significant length, any shaping rounds that might fall on Rounds 9-11 should be moved ahead to Round 8 of the pattern.

River Stitch (in the round over any number of sts)
Rounds 1-8: Knit.
Round 9: Purl.
Round 10: *K1 wrapping yarn 3 times, rep from * to end of rnd.
Round 11: Purl, dropping all extra wraps.
Rep Rnds 1-11 for pat.

1x1 Ribbing (in the round over an even number of sts)
All Rounds: *K1, P1; repeat from * to end of round.

Sewn Bind Off
Cut yarn at least 3 times longer than circumference to be bound off. Thread a yarn needle.
Step 1: Insert yarn needle & pull yarn through first 2 sts on left needle as if to purl.
Step 2: Insert tapestry needle knitwise through first st on left needle. Pull yarn through and remove first st from needle. One st BO.
Repeat steps 1 and 2 until all sts have been bound off.

Make 1 Increase (M1)
Pick up a st from the row below the working st on the LH needle. Knit into this st. One st inc.

DIRECTIONS
Body
Cast on 240 (272, 300, 332, 360, 392, 420, 452, 480) sts, PM to note beginning of the round and join for working in the round being careful not to twist sts.
Work 1x1 Ribbing until piece measures 2″ from CO.
Next Round: P120 (136, 150, 166, 180, 196, 210, 226, 240), place marker, P120 (136, 150, 166, 180, 196, 210, 226, 240).
Work in River Stitch for 22 rounds (2 repeats of pat). Piece should measure approximate-ly 5″ from CO.

Shape Waist
Work decrease and increase rnds on knit rnds only (Rnds 1-8 of River Stitch). If you are at a purled or elongated st rnd (rnds 9-11) work these as normal and continue with the decreases or increases on the next knit rnd.

Decrease Round: ssk, K2, ssk, K to 6 sts before next marker, K2tog, K2, K2tog, SM, K to end of rnd. 4 sts dec.
Continuing in River Stitch, work Decrease Round every 7th round twice more. 228 (260, 288, 320, 348, 380, 408, 440, 468) sts. Work even in River Stitch until piece measures 8″ from CO (you should have just finished rnd 11 of River Stitch).

Increase Round: M1, K2, M1, K to 2 sts before next marker, M1, K2, M1, SM, K to end of round. 4 sts inc.

Continuing in River Stitch, work Increase Round every 7th round twice more. 240 (272, 300, 332, 360, 392, 420, 452, 480) sts. Work even in River Stitch until piece measures 15.5 (15.5, 15.5, 15.5, 15.5, 15.5, 17, 17, 17)″ (9, 9, 9, 9, 9, 9, 10, 10, 10 total repeats of River Stitch) from CO, or desired length to underarms ending with rnd 11 of River Stitch.

Shape Armholes
(Remove markers as you work this rnd. 9 (13, 15, 16, 18, 19, 21, 22, 24) sts will be worked beyond the end of rnd.) K129 (149, 165, 182, 198, 215, 231, 248, 264), place just worked last 18 (26, 30, 32, 36, 38, 42, 44, 48) sts on scrap yarn, K120 (136, 150, 166, 180, 196, 210, 226, 240), place just worked last 18 (26, 30, 32, 36, 38, 42, 44, 48) sts on scrap yarn. Leaving Body sts on needles, set aside and work Sleeves.

Sleeves (make two)
The sleeves are worked in the rnd from the bottom up.
Cast on 80 (84, 92, 104, 116, 128, 140, 148, 152) sts loosely, PM, and join for working in the round being careful not to twist sts.
Work 1x1 Ribbing until piece measures 2″ from CO.
Next Round: Purl.
Work Rounds 1 to 11 of River Stitch.

Shape Armholes: Knit round and transfer the last 18 (26, 30, 32, 36, 38, 42, 44, 48)) sts onto scrap yarn leaving 62 (58, 62, 72, 80, 90, 98, 104, 104) live sleeve sts ready to join to body. Cut yarn and set sleeve aside.

Yoke
Sleeves and body are joined to work the upper portion of the sweater.
With yarn attached to the Body, K across 102 (110, 120, 134, 144, 158, 168, 182, 192) sts from body (back), K 62 (58, 62, 72, 80, 90, 98, 104, 104) sleeve sts, K 102 (110, 120, 134, 144, 158, 168, 182, 192) sts from body (front), K 62 (58, 62, 72, 80, 90, 98, 104, 104)) sts from remaining sleeve. Place marker for beginning of rnd. (This counts as Round 2 of River Stitch Pattern.) 329 (336, 364, 412, 448, 496, 532, 572, 592) sts.
Work 23 (23, 23, 27, 27, 34, 34, 38, 38) rnds in River Stitch.

Decrease Round 1: Decrease Round 1 is worked on round 4 (4, 4, 8, 8, 4, 4, 8, 8) of River Stitch pat: *K2, K2tog; rep from * to end of round. 82 (84, 91, 103, 112, 124, 132, 143, 148) sts dec. 246 (252, 273, 309, 336, 372, 399, 429, 444) sts.

Work 13 (13, 13, 17, 17, 19, 19, 21, 21) rnds even in River Stitch.
Decrease Round 2: Decrease Round 2 is worked on rnd 7 (7, 7, 4, 4, 2, 2, 8, 8) of River Stitch pat: *K1, K2tog; rep from * to end of rnd. 82 (84, 91, 103, 112, 124, 132, 143, 148) sts dec. 164 (168, 182, 206, 224, 248, 266, 286, 296) sts.
Work 11 (11, 11, 14, 14, 16, 16, 21, 21) rnds even in River Stitch.

Decrease Round 3: Decrease Round 3 is worked on rnd 8 of River Stitch pat: *K1, K2tog; rep from * to end of rnd. Some sizes will have 1 or 2 sts at the end of the round, K these. 54 (56, 60, 68, 74, 82, 88, 95, 98) sts dec. 110 (112, 122, 138, 150, 166, 178, 191, 198) sts. Purl 1 rnd, dec 1 st with a P2tog if you have an odd number of sts after the final decrease round.

For a smaller neck opening work rnds 10 & 11 of River Stitch,
repeat Decrease Round 3, and then continue to ribbing.
Work in 1x1 Ribbing for 1".
Bind off all sts using a sewn bind off.

Finishing

Graft together the held underarm sts of the body and sleeve
to form an invisible seam. Weave in ends, wash and block to
diagram.

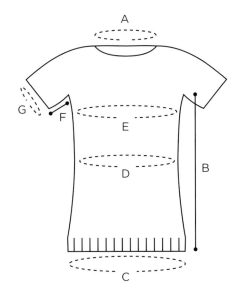

A 14.5 (15, 16.25, 18.5, 20, 22, 23.5, 25.5, 26.25)"
B 15.5 (15.5, 15.5, 15.5, 15.5, 15.5, 17, 17, 17)"
C 32 (36, 40, 44, 48, 52, 56, 60, 64)"
D 30.5 (34.5, 38.5, 42.5, 46.5, 50.5, 54.5, 58.5, 62.5)"
E 32 (36, 40, 44, 48, 52, 56, 60, 64)"
F 3.5" (all sizes)
G 10.5 (11.25, 12.25, 13.75, 15.5, 17, 18.5, 19.75, 20.25)"

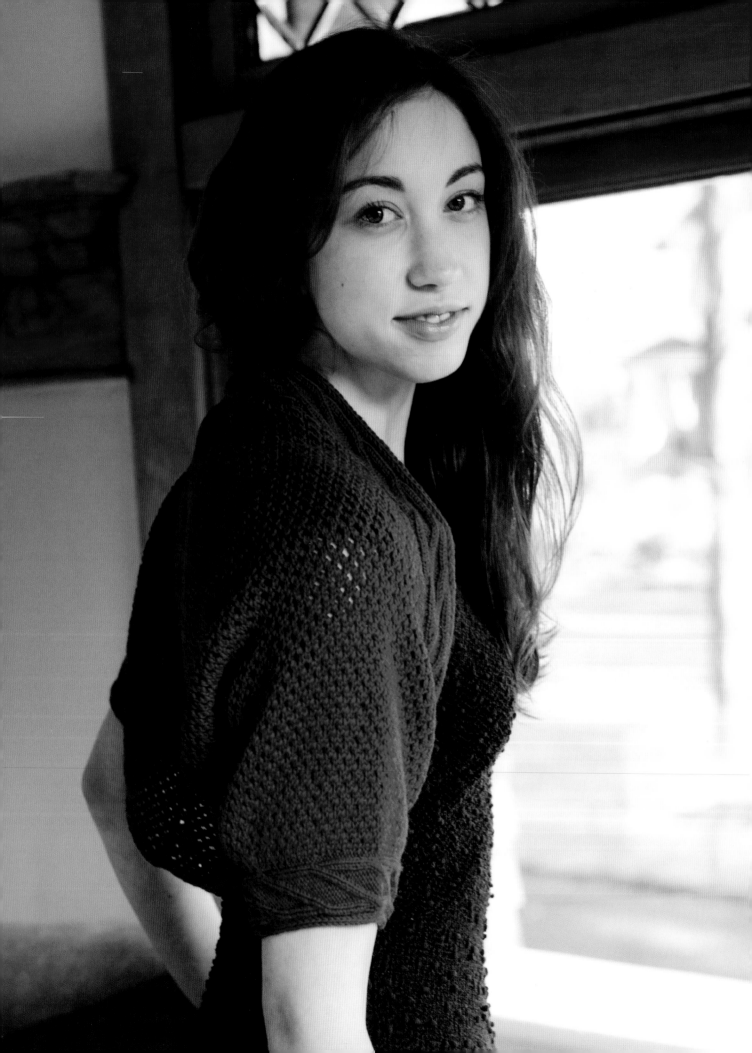

APIS SHRUG

by Heather Pfeifer

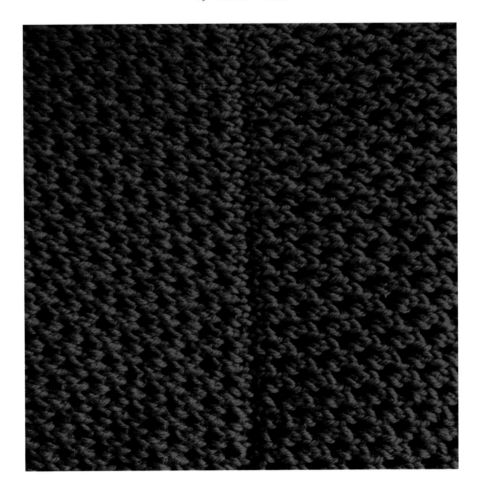

FINISHED MEASUREMENTS

Back width 16-18 (20-22, 24-26)", to fit bust measuring 32 (40, 48)"; garment is meant to be work with 0-4" positive ease

YARN

Knit Picks Stroll Sock Yarn (75% Superwash Merino Wool, 25% Nylon; 231 yards/50g): Everglade Heather 25607, 4 (5, 6) balls

NEEDLES

US 4 (3.5mm) 32 or 40" circular needle, or size to obtain St st gauge
US 3 (3.25mm) 32 or 40" circular needle, or size to obtain Chart A gauge

US 6 (4mm) One DPN or straight needle, for Bind Offs, or 2 sizes larger than St st gauge needle

GAUGE

24 sts and 32 rows = 4" in St st, blocked
20 sts and 16 rows = 2.5" x 1.5" over Chart A, blocked

NOTIONS

Yarn Needle
4 Split Ring Stitch Markers
Cable Needle
Scrap Yarn or Stitch Holder

Apis Shrug

Notes:

A graceful, travelling twisted pattern at each cuff starts and finishes this classy shrug. The body of simple honeycomb lace lends a touch of elegance to an everyday accessory for all-season layering.

Beginning with the sleeves, each cuff is knit flat. Stitches are then picked up along one edge to work the Honeycomb Lace up the sleeve to mid-back, where the sleeves are attached with a three-needle bind off. The cuff and sleeves are then seamed to the underarm. Stitches are picked up along the entire circumference of the shrug to work an applied i-cord and edging to match the cuffs.

This pattern is ideal for knitting both pieces of the shrug at once, but not in the round. Due to the stretch of the Honeycomb Lace pattern, each size will fit a variety of body types. If you like it more form-fitting or are between sizes, go down one size. If you want 2-4" positive ease to layer over any top, stay with the size closest matching your back measurement.

Honeycomb Lace (worked flat over odd number of sts)

The pattern is worked by increasing on the RS (yo twice) and decreasing those stitches on the WS (P2tog), that is: the first P2tog is worked using a purl stitch and 1 yo; the second P2tog uses 1 yo and a purl st.

Row 1 (RS): K1, (K2, yo twice) to last 2 sts, K2.
Row 2 (WS): P1, (P2tog) to last 2 sts, P2.
Row 3: K2, (yo twice, K2) to last st, K1.
Row 4: P2, (P2tog) to last st, P1.
Rep Rows 1-4 for pat.

3-Needle Bind-off

Hold the two pieces of knitting with right sides together and the needle tips facing to the right. Insert a third needle (using largest size) into the first st on each of the needles Kwise, starting with the front needle. Knit the st on the front needle together with the st on the back needle. Repeat this motion, inserting your needle into one st on the front and back needles, knitting them together and slipping them off of the needles.

Each time you complete a second st, pass the first finished st over the second and off of the needle (as you would in a traditional BO). As you progress along the sts you will see the seam begin to appear.

Before working charts, read instructions for pattern repeats and special instructions. The RS chart rows (odd numbers) are worked from right to left, and WS chart rows (even numbers, from left to right.)

Twist 3 Right (T3R): Hold 1 st to the back on CN, K2, P1 from CN.
2 over 1 Right Cross (2/1RC): Hold 1 st to the back on CN, K2, K1 from CN.

Purl Front and Back (PFB): P next st but do not remove original st from needle, P into back loop of same st. Slide to right needle. 1 st inc.

Make One Purlwise (M1P): PU strand between sts from front to back with left needle, purl through the back loop. 1 st inc.

Right Lifted Increase (RLI): Insert right needle into stitch below first stitch on left needle. K this stitch. 1 st inc.

Chart A, worked over 20 sts

Row 1 (RS): k1, p2, k2, p5, t3r, k2, p2, k3.
Row 2 (WS): Sl 3 wyif, k2, p2, k1, p2, k5, p2, k2, p1.
Row 3: k1, p2, k2, p4, t3r, p1, k2, p2, k3.
Row 4: Sl 3 wyif, (k2, p2) twice, k4, p2, k2, p1.
Row 5: k1, p2, k2, p3, t3r, (p2, k2) twice, k1.
Row 6: Sl 3 wyif, k2, p2, (k3, p2) twice, k2, p1.
Row 7: k1, p2, k2, p2, t3r, p3, k2, p2, k3.
Row 8: Sl 3 wyif, k2, p2, k4, (p2, k2) twice, p1.
Row 9: k1, p2, k2, p1, t3r, p4, k2, p2, k3.
Row 10: Sl 3 wyif, k2, p2, k5, (p2, k1) twice, k1, p1.
Row 11: k1, p2, k2, t3r, p5, k2, p2, k3.
Row 12: Sl 3 wyif, k2, p2, k6, p4, k2, p1.
Row 13: k1, p2, k1, t3r, p5, 2/1RC, p2, k3.
Row 14: Sl 3 wyif, k2, p3, k6, p3, k2, p1.
Row 15: k1, p2, t3r, p5, 2/1RC, k1, p2, k3.
Row 16: Sl 3 wyif, k2, p4, k6, p2, k2, p1.

Chart B (Increasing) P2tog with 1 st from Body

Row 1 (RS): Sl 3 wyib, pfb, p2tog, turn.
Row 2 (WS): k3, p3.
Row 3: Sl 3 wyib, pfb, p1, p2tog, turn.
Row 4: k4, p3.
Row 5: Sl 3 wyib, pfb, p2, p2tog, turn.
Row 6: (k2, p1) twice, p2.
Row 7: Sl 3 wyib, p2, rli, k1, p1, p2tog, turn.
Row 8: (k2, p2) twice, p1.
Row 9: Sl 3 wyib, p2, rli, k2, p1, p2tog, turn.
Row 10: (k2, p3) twice.
Row 11: Sl 3 wyib, p2, rli, k3, p1, p2tog, turn.
Row 12: k2, p4, k2, p3.
Row 13: Sl 3 wyib, p2, k2, M1P, k2, p1, p2tog, turn.
Row 14: k2, p2, K1, p2, k2, p3.
Row 15: Sl 3 wyib, p2, k2, M1P, p1, k2, p1, p2tog, turn.
Row 16: (k2, p2) three times, p1.
Row 17: Sl 3 wyib, p2, k2, M1P, p2, k2, p1, p2tog, turn.
Row 18: k2, p2, K3, P2, K2, P3.
Row 19: Sl 3 wyib, p2, k2, M1P, p3, k2, p1, p2tog, turn.
Row 20: k2, p2, K4, P2, K2, P3.
Row 21: Sl 3 wyib, p2, k2, M1P, p4, k2, p1, p2tog, turn.
Row 22: k2, p2, k5, p2, k2, p3.
Row 23: Sl 3 wyib, p2, k2, M1P, p5, k2, p1, p2tog, turn.
Row 24: k2, p2, k6, p2, k2, p3.
Row 25: Sl 3 wyib, p2, k2, M1P, p5, 2/1RC, p1, p2tog, turn.
Row 26: k2, p3, k6, p2, k2, p3.
Row 27: Sl 3 wyib, p2, k2, M1P, p5, 2/1RC, k1, p1, p2tog, turn.
Row 28: k2, p4, k6, p2, k2, p3.

Chart C (Cable Edging), P2tog with 1 st from Body

Row 1 (RS): Sl 3 wyib, p2, k2, p5, t3r, k2, p1, p2tog, turn.
Row 2 (WS): k2, p2, k1, p2, k5, p2, k2, p3.
Row 3: Sl 3 wyib, p2, k2, p4, t3r, p1, k2, p1, p2tog, turn.
Row 4: (k2, p2) twice, k4, p2, k2, p3.

Row 5: Sl 3 wyib, p2, k2, p3, t3r, p2, k2, p1, p2tog, turn.
Row 6: k2, p2, (k3, p2) twice, k2, p3.
Row 7: Sl 3 wyib, p2, k2, p2, t3r, p3, k2, p1, p2tog, turn.
Row 8: k2, p2, k4, (p2, k2) twice, p3.
Row 9: Sl 3 wyib, p2, k2, p1, t3r, p4, k2, p1, p2tog, turn.
Row 10: k2, p2, k5, p2, k1, p2, k2, p3.
Row 11: Sl 3 wyib, p2, k2, t3r, p5, k2, p1, p2tog, turn.
Row 12: k2, p2, k6, p4, k2, p3.
Row 13: Sl 3 wyib, p2, k1, t3r, p5, 2/1rc, p1, p2tog, turn.
Row 14: k2, p3, k6, p3, k2, p3.
Row 15: Sl 3 wyib, p2, t3r, p5, 2/1rc, k1, p1, p2tog, turn.
Row 16: k2, p4, k6, p2, k2, p3.

Chart D (Decreasing), P2tog with 1 st from Body before turn
Row 1 (RS): Sl 3 wyib, p2, k1, t3r, p4, p2tog, k2, p1, p2tog, turn.
Row 2 (WS): k2, p2, k6, p3, k2, p3.
Row 3: Sl 3 wyib, p2, t3r, p4, p2tog, k2, p1, p2tog, turn.
Row 4: k2, p2, k6, p2, k2, p3.
Row 5: Sl 3 wyib, p2, k2, p4, p2tog, k2, p1, p2tog, turn.
Row 6: k2, p2, k5, p2, k2, p3.
Row 7: Sl 3 wyib, p2, k2, p3, p2tog, k2, p1, p2tog, turn.
Row 8: K2, P2, K4, P2, K2, p3.
Row 9: Sl 3 wyib, p2, k2, p2, p2tog, k2, p1, p2tog, turn.
Row 10: k2, p2, k3, p2, k2, p3.
Row 11: Sl 3 wyib, p2, k2, p1, p2tog, k2, p1, p2tog, turn.
Row 12: (k2, p2) three times, p1.
Row 13: Sl 3 wyib, p2, k2, p2tog, k2, p1, p2tog, turn.
Row 14: k2, p2, k1, p2, k2, p3.
Row 15: Sl 3 wyib, p2, k2, k2tog, k1, p1, p2tog, turn.
Row 16: k2, p4, k2, p3.
Row 17: Sl 3 wyib, p2, k2, k2tog, p1, p2tog, turn.
Row 18: (k2, p3) twice.
Row 19: Sl 3 wyib, p2, k1, k2tog, p1, p2tog, turn.
Row 20: (k2, p2) twice, p1.
Row 21: Sl 3 wyib, p2, k2tog, p1, p2tog, turn.
Row 22: k5, p3.
Row 23: Sl 3 wyib, p2, p2tog twice, turn.
Row 24: k4, p3.
Row 25: Sl 3 wyib, p1, p2tog twice, turn.
Row 26: k3, p3.
Row 27: Sl 3 wyib, p2tog twice, turn.
Row 28: k2, p3.

Chart E: Right Back
Row 1: K1, (K2, yo twice) to last 2 sts, K2.
Row 2: P1, (P2tog) to last 2 sts, P2.
Row 3: K2, (yo twice, K2) to last st, K1.
Row 4: P2, (P2tog) to last st, P1.
Rows 5-8: Rep Rows 1-4.
Row 9: K1, (K2, yo twice) to last 2 sts, K1, yo, K1.
Row 10: P2, (P2tog) to last 2 sts, P2.
Row 11: K2, (yo twice, K2) to last 2 sts, yo, K2.
Row 12: P4, (P2tog) to last st, P1.

Chart F: Left Back
Row 1: K1, (K2, yo twice) to last 2 sts, K2.
Row 2: P1, (P2tog) to last 2 sts, P2.
Row 3: K2, (yo twice, K2) to last st, K1.

Row 4: P2, (P2tog) to last st, P1.
Rows 5-8: Rep Rows 1-4.
Row 9: K1, yo, (K2, yo twice) to last 2 sts, K2.
Row 10: P1, (P2tog) to last 3 sts, P3.
Row 11: K1, yo, K2, (yo twice, K2) to last st, K1.
Row 12: P2, (P2tog) to last 3 sts, P3.

DIRECTIONS

Knit the two pieces of the shrug simultaneously to ensure identical shaping.

Cuffs (make 2 identical)

Using US 3 (3.25mm) needle, or Chart A gauge needle, CO 20 sts, leaving 12" tail to seam cuff.

Setup Row (WS): P3, K2, P4, K6, P2, K2, P1.
Work Rows 1-16 of Chart A 7 (9, 11) times. Piece measures approximately 10.5 (13.5, 16.5)" along the I-cord (formed by the 3 slipped sts) at the left edge.
Bind off loosely in pattern. Cut yarn, leaving a 16" tail for seaming from cuff to underarm.

Sleeves

Note: These are worked flat. Using smallest needle, with RS facing and the I-cord edge (formed by the 3 slipped sts) at the bottom, begin at the right top corner and PU 2 sts for every 3 rows, for a total of 75 (95, 115) sts.
Change to larger needles.
Setup Row (WS): P to end.
Work Rows 1-4 of Honeycomb Lace 9 (10, 11) times, until piece measures 7.5 (8.25, 8.75)" from I-cord edge.

Underarm Shaping

With RS facing, place split ring marker 6 (10, 14) sts from the left edge of each piece to mark underarm BO. It is important to bind off sts very loosely; use the needle 2 sizes larger than Honeycomb gauge needle.
Next Row (RS): BO 6 (10, 14) sts Kwise, 1 st will be on right needle, (K2, yo twice) to 2 sts before marker, k2, remove marker, K6 (10, 14) sts.
Next Row (WS): BO 6 (10, 14) sts Pwise, 1 st will be on right needle, (P2tog) to last 2 sts, P2. 63 (75, 87) sts.
Next Row: Work Row 3 of Honeycomb Lace pattern.
Next Row: Work Row 4 of Honeycomb Lace pattern.

Back Shaping

Work Rows 1-12 of Right Back (Chart E) on one piece and Left Back (Chart F) on the other 4 (5, 6) times total, continuing in Honeycomb Lace pattern between charts as established. 2 sts inc each rep per piece. 71 (85, 99) sts.

Work Rows 1-4 of Right and Left Back (Charts E and F) 3 (5, 6) times, continuing in Honeycomb Lace pattern between charts as established, until piece measures approximately 18.25 (20.5, 23)" from cuff, or until length from Cuff reaches your mid-back. Do not break yarn.

Repeat all instructions from Cuff for second side, if both pieces weren't worked concurrently. Do not break yarn. Piece now measures approximately 18.25 (20.5, 23)" from cuff.

Joining

Place right sides facing, ensuring the pieces are symmetrical, and work a 3-Needle Bind Off using the largest needles.
Cut only the yarn used for the BO.
Seam cuff. Seam sleeves from cuff to underarm using tail from cuff.

Edging

Specific counts are provided here. However, if you prefer to customize the placement of where the twisted pattern begins on the edging, a step-by-step tutorial for calculation is provided. To customize, skip over the Non-Customizable Version and go straight to the Step-By-Step Customizable Version.

Non-Customizable Version

Using larger needle, and with RS facing, beginning at the top mid-back and working around the entire piece, pick up and knit 3 sts for every 4 rows along the length and 1 st in each underarm stitch. You should have a total of 236 (272, 332) sts.

Lay the piece out so the opening is facing up. Working clockwise from the top mid-back seam, place marker A 33 (35, 49) sts to the right of the seam, and marker D 33 (35, 49) sts to the left of the seam

Place marker B 14 sts to the right of marker A, and marker C 14 sts to the left of marker D.
You will have 142 (174, 206) sts between markers B and C.

Customizable Version

Try the shrug on to determine the placement for the cabled edging to begin on each side.
Place markers A & D equal sts from top mid-back seam where the cables will begin.

Ensure that there are 14 sts between markers A & B, and markers C & D, and that the number of sts between markers B and C is a multiple of 8 sts + 6.

Your stitch counts are now set to begin the edging as follows:

Basic I-Cord Edging:

Note: At the end of each RS row, the P2tog will P 1 st from edging together with 1 st from body.
Beginning at top mid-back, K1 to join in the round, then using the cable cast on method, CO 5 sts.
Setup Row 1: K3, P1, P2tog (1 st from edging, 1 st from body), turn.
Setup Row 2: K2, P3.
Now work the following 2 rows:
Row 1: Sl 3 wyib, P1, P2tog, turn.
Row 2: K2, P3.
Repeat Rows 1-2 to marker A. Remove marker.

Work Chart B (increasing) to marker B. Remove marker.
Work Chart C (cable edging) around the bottom to marker C. On the final repeat only work Rows 1-12. Remove marker.

Work Chart D (decreasing) to marker D. Remove marker.

Continue Basic I-Cord Edging to the mid-back seam as follows:
Row 1: Slip 3 wyib, P1, P2tog, turn.
Row 2: K2, P3.

Finishing

Seam 5 sts of edging together.
Weave in ends, gently block according to the diagram, without over-stretching the Honeycomb Lace.

Legend

 knit
RS: knit stitch
WS: purl stitch

purl
RS: purl stitch
WS: knit stitch

twist 3 right
sl1 to CN, hold in back. k2, p1 from CN

 purl front back
purl next st but do not remove original st from needle, P into back loop of same st. Slide to right needle. 1 st inc.

 k2tog
RS: Knit two stitches together as one stitch
WS: Purl 2 stitches tog

 slip
RS: Slip stitch as if to purl, holding yarn in back
WS: Slip stitch as if to purl, holding yarn in front

2/1 right cross
sl1 to CN, hold in back. k2, k1 from CN

 p2tog
RS: Purl 2 stitches together
WS: Knit 2 stitches together

yo twice
yarn over twice

 make one right
Insert right needle into stitch below first stitch on left needle. K this stitch. 1 st inc

ssk
RS: Sl 1 st as if to knit, sl another st as if to knit. Insert left-hand needle into front of these 2 stitches and knit tog

WS: Purl 2 sts together in back loops, inserting needle from the left, behind and into the backs of the 2nd & 1st sts in that order

 make one purlwise
PU strand between sts from front to back with left needle, purl through the back loop

yo
yarn over

k2
represents two individual sts but is shown as one on the chart

Chart A

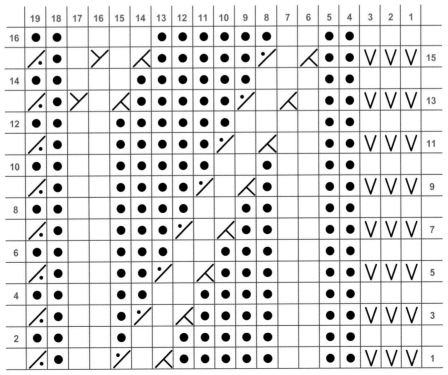

Chart C

Chart B

19	18	17	16	15	14	13	12	11	10	9	8	7	6	5	4	3	2	1	
•	•					•	•	•	•	•	•			•	•				28
/.	•		Y		Λ	•	•	•	•	•	M			•	•	V	V	V	27
•	•			•		•	•	•	•	•			•	•					26
/.	•		Y		Λ	•	•	•	•	•	M		•	•	V	V	V		25
•	•					•	•	•	•			•	•						24
/.	•					•	•	•	M		•	•	V	V	V				23
•	•					•	•	•			•	•							22
/.	•					•	•	M		•	•	V	V	V					21
•	•					•	•			•	•								20
/.	•					•	M		•	•	V	V	V						19
•	•					•	•		•	•									18
/.	•					M		•	•	V	V	V							17
•	•				•			•	•										16
/.	•				M		•	•	V	V	V								15
•	•					•	•												14
/.	•					•	•	V	V	V									13
•	•				•	•													12
/.	•			MR	•	•	V	V	V										11
•	•			•	•														10
/.	•		MR	•	•	V	V	V											9
•	•			•	•														8
/.	•	MR	•	•	V	V	V												7
•	•		•	•															6
/.	•	•	Y	V	V	V													5
•	•	•	•																4
/.	•	Y	V	V	V														3
•	•	•																	2
/.	Y	V	V	V															1

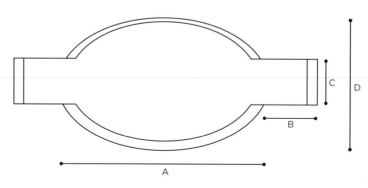

A 20.25 (23.5, 28.25)"
B 7.5 (8.25, 8.75)"
C 10.5 (13.5, 16.5)"
D 15 (17, 19.5)"

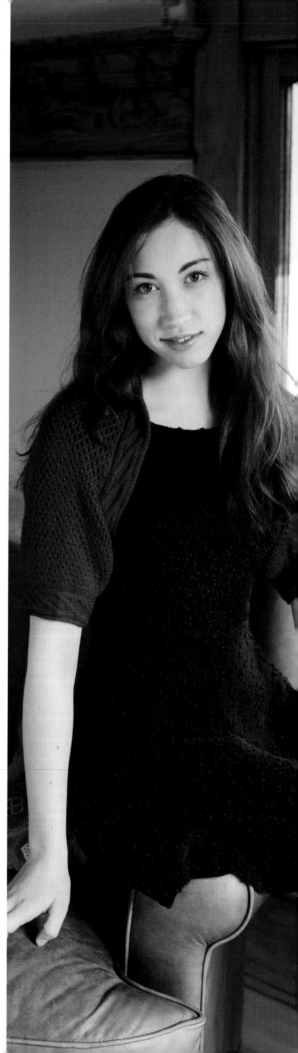

Chart D

	18	17	16	15	14	13	12	11	10	9	8	7	6	5	4	3	2	1	

Rows numbered 28, 26, 24, 22, 20, 18, 16, 14, 12, 10, 8, 6, 4, 2 on the left and 27, 25, 23, 21, 19, 17, 15, 13, 11, 9, 7, 5, 3, 1 on the right.

Chart E

	11	10	9	8	7	6	5	4	3	2	1	

Rows numbered 12, 10, 8, 6, 4, 2 on the left and 11, 9, 7, 5, 3, 1 on the right.

The k2 symbol represents two individual sts but is shown as one on the charts

Chart F

	11	10	9	8	7	6	5	4	3	2	1	

Rows numbered 12, 10, 8, 6, 4, 2 on the left and 11, 9, 7, 5, 3, 1 on the right.

NAUTICAL PULLOVER

by Ann Weaver

FINISHED MEASUREMENTS

40 (44, 48, 52, 56, 60, 64, 68, 72)" finished bust measurement; garment is meant to be worn with 8" of positive ease.

YARN

Knit Picks Gloss Lace (70% Merino Wool, 30% Silk; 440 yards/50g):
Sterling 24182 (A), Natural 24178 (B); 2 (2, 2, 3, 3, 3, 3, 4, 4) hanks each

NEEDLES

US 7 (4.5mm) 32" or longer circular needle depending on size, plus 2 DPN's for i-cord and 3-Needle BO, or size to obtain gauge

NOTIONS

Yarn Needle
2 Stitch Markers
Stitch Holder or Waste Yarn

GAUGE

16 sts and 26 rows = 4" in St st, blocked.

Nautical Pullover

Notes:

This lightweight, oversized pullover is knit in two pieces from the bottom up. The dolman sleeves are knit as part of the body. The side seams provide stability and keep the lightweight fabric from stretching and becoming misshapen. The neck is edged in two-color i-cord.

Wrap & Turn (W&T)

Work until the stitch to be wrapped. If knitting: Bring yarn to the front of the work, slip next st as if to purl, return the yarn to the back; turn work and slip wrapped st onto RH needle. Continue across row. If purling: Bring yarn to the back of the work, slip next st as if to purl, return the yarn to the front; turn work and slip wrapped st onto RH needle. Continue across row.

Picking up wraps: Work to the wrapped st. If knitting, insert the RH needle under the wrap(s), then through the wrapped st kwise. Knit the wrap(s) together with the wrapped st. If purling, slip the wrapped st pwise onto the RH needle, and use the LH needle to lift the wrap(s) and place them on the RH needle. Slip wrap(s) and unworked st back to LH needle; purl all together through the back loop.

3-Needle Bind Off

* Hold the two pieces of knitting together with the points facing to the right. Insert a third needle into the first stitch on each of the needles Kwise, starting with the front needle. Work a knit st, pulling the loop through both of the sts you've inserted the third needle through. After pulling the loop through, sl the first st off of each of the needles. Repeat from *. Pass the first finished st over the second and off of the needle.

DIRECTIONS

Front

The front is worked flat in one piece from the bottom up. The fronts of the sleeves are worked as part of the body.

Hem

*Using A, loosely CO 80 (88, 96, 104, 112, 120, 128, 136, 144) sts. Knit 10 rows.

Body

Begin working in St st (K on RS, P on WS), beginning with a RS knit row. Work 22 rows in St st. Cut A and join B.
Using B, work 26 rows in St st. Cut B and join A.
Using A, work 26 rows in St st. Cut A and join B.
Using B, work 14 rows in St st.

Sleeves

Continue to work in St st. At the end of the next two rows, place marker and CO 8 sts using the backward loop cast on. 96 (104, 112, 120, 128, 136, 144, 152, 160) sts.

CO 8 sts at the end of the next 10 rows—12 increase rows total (6 on each side); 48 sleeves sts on each side; 176 (184, 192, 200, 208, 216, 224, 232, 240) sts total.

Sleeves and Body

Cut B and join A. Begin working in garter stitch (K every row) for the rest of the front. Using A, knit 32 rows.

Cut A and join B. Using B, knit 32 rows.
Cut B and join A. Using A, knit 0 (0, 4, 4, 8, 8, 12, 12, 16) rows.*

Shape Neck and Shoulders

Divide front at neck and shape neck and shoulders as follows:
Row 1 (RS): K78 (80, 84, 86, 89, 93, 97, 100, 104), BO 20 (24, 24, 28, 30, 30, 30, 32, 32), knit to end—78 (80, 84, 86, 89, 93, 97, 100, 104) sts each sleeve/shoulder.
Row 2 (WS): Work to gap; join a second skein of A, BO 4 sts at left neckline, work to last 8 sts, w&t.
Row 3: Work to gap; BO 4 sts at right neckline, work to last 8 sts, w&t.
Row 4: Work to gap; BO 4, work to 8 sts before last wrapped st, w&t.
Rows 5–7: Rep Row 4—6 shaping rows total; 66 (68, 72, 74, 77, 81, 85, 88, 92) sts each sleeve/shoulder.
Row 8: Work to gap; k1, ssk, work to 8 sts before last wrapped st, w&t.
Rows 9–13: Rep Row 8—63 (65, 69, 71, 74, 78, 82, 85, 89) sts each sleeve/shoulder.
Row 14: Work to gap; work all sts, working wraps together with wrapped sts.
Row 15: Rep Row 14.
Keep sts live on needle or place on stitch holder or length of waste yarn. The front will be joined to the back at the shoulders using the 3-Needle Bind Off.

Back

Work as for front from * to *.

Shape Neck and Shoulders

Divide back at neck and shape neck and shoulders as follows:
Row 1 (RS): Work to last 8 sts, w&t.
Row 2 (WS): Rep Row 1.
Rows 3–8: Work to 8 sts before last wrapped st, w&t.
Row 9: K33 (35, 39, 41, 44, 48, 52, 55, 59), BO 46 (50, 50, 54, 56, 56, 56, 58, 58), knit to 8 sts before last wrapped st, w&t—65 (67, 71, 73, 76, 80, 84, 87, 91) sts each sleeve/shoulder (including wrapped sts).
Row 10: Work to gap; join a second skein of A, K1, ssk, work to 8 sts before last wrapped st, w&t.
Rows 11–13: Rep Row 10—63 (65, 69, 71, 74, 78, 82, 85, 89) sts each sleeve/shoulder.
Row 14: Work to gap; work all sts, working wraps together with wrapped sts.
Row 15: Rep Row 14.

Join Front and Back

Using A, holding RSs together, using dpn and beginning at either cuff, bind off using 3-Needle BO, knitting together 1 st from each needle, to neck opening. Rejoin A and work bind off from neck opening to cuff.

Finishing

Weave in ends, wash and block to diagram. Sew side seams.

Neck Edging

Using A, using circ needle and beginning at back right shoulder, PU and K 50 (54, 54, 58, 60, 60, 60, 62, 62) sts evenly spaced along back neck and 54 (58, 58, 62, 60, 68, 68, 74, 74) sts evenly spaced along front neck—104 (112, 112, 120, 120, 128, 128, 136, 136) sts.

Using A and DPN, CO 4 sts. Work attached i-cord edging as follows:

I-Cord Round: With RS facing, K3, sl 1 kwise, yo, K1 from the sts picked up along the neck edge, pass slipped st and yo over, then slide sts to opposite end of needle.

Using A, work 4 rnds of attached i-cord. Join B but do not cut A. Work 4 rnds using B, carrying A along back of work.

Repeat the previous 8 rnds 12 (13, 13, 14, 14, 15, 15, 16, 16) more times; all picked-up sts used.

Graft 4 remaining sts to CO sts, or BO and sew 4 remaining sts to CO sts. Weave in ends.

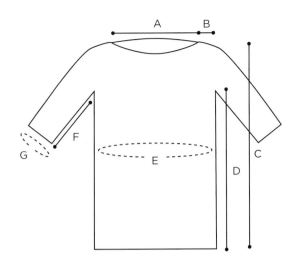

A 12.5 (13.5, 13.5, 14.5, 15, 15, 15, 15.5, 15.5)"
B 3.75, (4.25, 5.25, 5.75, 6.5, 7.5, 8.5, 9.25, 10.75)"
C 26 (26, 26.5, 26.5, 27, 27, 27.5, 27.5, 28)"
D 14" (all sizes)
E 40 (44, 48, 52, 56, 60, 64, ,68, 72)"
F 11" (all sizes)
G 8 (8, 8.5, 8.5, 9, 9, 9.5, 9.5, 10)"

STRAND HILL CARDIGAN

by Keya Kuhn

FINISHED MEASUREMENTS

31 (36, 40, 44, 48, 50.25)″ finished bust measurement (blocked); garment is meant to be worn with 2″ positive ease

YARN

Knit Picks Stroll (75% Superwash Merino Wool, 25% Nylon; 231 yards/50g); Dogwood Heather 25603, 3 (3, 4, 4, 5, 6) balls

NEEDLES

US 8 (5mm) 32″ or longer circular needle, DPNs or 16″ circular needle, or size to obtain gauge

NOTIONS

Yarn Needle
10 Non-locking Stitch Markers (4 of one color; 6 of a second color)
Waste Yarn

GAUGE

22 sts and 26 rows = 4″ in stockinette stitch, blocked

Strand Hill Cardigan

Notes:

This cardigan is a top-down, seamless pattern that includes a delicate complement of Estonian lace on the front and back panels. This pattern is meant to be worn with two inches of positive ease across the bust; you may wish to choose your actual bust measurement if you prefer a more close-fitting style. This pattern is fully charted and is worked flat. It will be necessary to refer to the charts while working the written instructions. When using the charts, read RS rows (odd numbers) from right to left, and WS rows (even numbers) from left to right.

The initial markers used in the Yoke section should be 4 markers of the same color as mentioned in the Notions section, above. The remaining 6 markers will be used later to mark the lace panel sections of the work.

If it is necessary for your body type to increase the length of the raglan seam, do so before beginning the Front Panel Lace section.

Sleeve Cuffs: Work in the round as a continuation of the sleeve.

Knitted Cast On

Turn work to WS, CO 1 (2, 2, 4, 4) sts by knitting into the last st and placing the new st back onto the left-hand needle.

Inc1R: K into the front of the st, then K into the opening of the front of the st below it; slide original st off of the left-hand needle.

Inc1L: K into the front of the st below the st on the left-hand needle, then K into the front of the st on the needle; slide original st off of the left-hand needle.

DIRECTIONS

Yoke

Using a long-tail method, CO 33 (39, 45, 51, 55, 61) sts.

Yoke Set-up Row (WS): P2 (2, 3, 3, 4, 4) sts for Front, PM, P3 (5, 5, 7, 6, 8) sts for Sleeve, PM, P23 (25, 29, 31, 35, 37) sts for Back, PM, P3 (5, 5, 7, 6, 8) sts for Sleeve, PM, P2 (2, 3, 3, 4, 4) sts for Front.

Raglan Increase Rows

Row 1 (RS): *K to 1st before marker, Inc1R, SM, Inc1L; repeat from * across row to end. 8 sts inc.

Row 2 and all even rows for Yoke: P, slipping markers as you come to them.

Row 3: Repeat Row 1. 8 sts inc. 49 (55, 61, 67, 71, 77) sts.

Row 5: K to 1st before marker, Inc1R, SM, Inc1L, K to 1st before marker, Inc1R, SM, Inc1L, K 0 (1, 3, 4, 6, 7), PM of a different color, work Row 1 of Lace Chart A across 25 stitches, PM of a different color, K 1 (2, 4, 5, 7, 8), Inc1R, SM, Inc1L, K to 1st before marker, Inc1R, SM, Inc1L, K to end.

Row 7: K to 1st before marker, Inc1R, SM, Inc1L, K to 1st before marker, Inc1R, SM, Inc1L, K to marker, SM, work Row 3 of Lace Chart A, SM, K to 1st before marker, *Inc1R, SM, Inc1L*, K to 1st before marker, rep from * to *, K to end. 8 sts inc.

Rows 9, 11, 13, 15: Continue to work Raglan Increase Rows as established in Row 7, working subsequent Chart A rows. 8 sts inc each row.

Row 16: P across row, slipping markers as you come to them. 97 (103, 109, 115, 119, 125) sts after 1st completion of Rows 1-16; 10 (10, 11, 11, 12, 12) sts each Front, 19 (21, 21, 23, 22, 24) sts each Sleeve, 39 (41, 45, 47, 51, 53) sts for Back.

Repeat rows 5-16 for 3 (4, 5, 5, 6, 6) total repeats; total stitch count equals 193 (247, 301, 307, 359, 365) sts. Each front will have 22 (28, 35, 35, 42, 42) sts; each sleeve will have 43 (57, 69, 71, 82, 84) sts; the back will have 63 (77, 93, 95, 111, 113) sts.

Front Panel Lace

Beginning on the RS, continue working Back and Sleeves in established pattern. AT THE SAME TIME, begin working Lace Chart B across the front panels thus:

Row 1 (RS): K4 (7, 11, 11, 14, 14), PM, work Lace Chart B (Row 1) across 13 sts, PM, K to 1 st before marker, Inc1R, SM, Inc1L, K to 1 st before marker, Inc1R, SM, Inc1L, K to marker, SM, work Lace Chart A (Row 1), SM, K to 1 st before marker, Inc1R, SM, Inc1L, K to 1 st before marker, Inc1R, SM, Inc1L, K4 (7, 10, 10, 14, 14) sts, PM, work Lace Chart B (Row 1) across 13 sts, PM, K4 (7, 11, 11, 14, 14). 8 sts inc.

Row 2 (WS): P across row, slipping markers as you come to them.

Row 3: K to marker, SM, work Lace Chart B (Row 3) across 13 sts, SM, K to 1 st before marker, Inc1R, SM, Inc1L, K to 1 st before marker, Inc1R, SM, Inc1L, K to marker, SM, work Lace Chart A (Row 3), SM, K to 1 st before marker, Inc1R, SM, Inc1L, K to 1 st before marker, Inc1R, SM, Inc1L, K to marker, SM, work Lace Chart B (Row 3) across 13 sts, SM, K to end of row. 8 sts inc.

Row 4: P across row, slipping markers as you come to them.

Continue in the pattern established by Rows 3 and 4 through Row 12 of both Lace Chart A and Lace Chart B. Each front will have 28 (34, 41, 41, 48, 48) sts; each sleeve will have 55 (69, 81, 83, 94, 96) sts; the back will have 75 (89, 105, 107, 123, 125) sts. Total sts 241 (295, 349, 355, 407, 413).

Divide for Body

Row 1 (RS): K to marker, SM, work Lace Chart B (Row 1), SM, K to marker, remove marker without increasing, CO 0 (2, 2, 4, 4, 5) sts using knitted CO method, place sleeve sts on waste yarn, remove marker without increasing, K to next marker, SM, work Lace Chart A (Row 1), SM, K to marker, remove marker without increasing, CO 0 (2, 2, 4, 4, 5) sts using knitted CO method, place sleeve sts on waste yarn, remove marker without increasing, K to next marker, SM, work Lace Chart B (Row 1), SM, K to end. Total sts remaining on needle: 131 (161, 191, 197, 227, 231) sts.

Row 2 (WS): P across front and back panels, including CO sts of the previous row, slipping markers as you come to them.

Row 3: K to marker, SM, work Lace Chart B, SM, K to marker, SM, work Lace Chart A, SM, K to marker, SM, work Lace Chart B, SM, K to end.

Continue to work in this manner, following the front and back panel lace charts and knitting all RS sts between lace panels and purling all WS sts until work measures approximately 10.75 (12.75, 12.75, 14.25, 14.25, 14.25, 15.75)" from underarm; end having completed Row 12 of both charts.

Bottom Edging

Row 1 (RS): K across all sts, removing markers as you come to them.

Row 2 (WS): P across all sts.

Rows 3 and 6: K1, *P1, K1; rep from * across.

Rows 4 and 5: P1, *K1, P1; rep from * across.

Repeat Row 4.

BO loosely in established pattern.

Collar/Front Bands

With RS facing, using the longer of the two circular needles and beginning at the lower corner of the right front panel, PU and K 3 sts for every 4 rows along the right front edge, 1 st for every st along the neck, then 3 sts for every 4 rows long the left front edge, ending at the lower left front corner with an odd number of stitches.

Beginning with a WS row, work the following pattern:

Row 1 (WS): P across all sts, removing markers as you come to them.

Row 2 (RS): K1, *P1, K1; rep from * across row.

Rows 3 and 6 (WS): K1, *P1, K1; rep from * across row.

Rows 4 and 5 (RS): P1, *K1, P1; rep from * across row.

Sizes 32 (36, 40, 44): Repeat Rows 3-6 once more, then Row 3.

Sizes 48 and 52: Repeat Rows 3-6 twice, then Row 3.

Bind off (RS) in the existing pattern stitch.

Sleeves

Place 55 (69, 81, 83, 94, 96) held sts of one sleeve on 16″ circular needle or DPN's, removing waste yarn completely. Beginning at the center of the underarm, PU and K0 (1, 1, 2, 2, 3) sts from underarm selvage, K across sleeve stitches, PU and K0 (1, 1, 2, 1, 2) sts from underarm selvage; one round completed. 55 (71, 83, 87, 97, 101) sts.

Joining sleeve sts to work in the round, K three additional rounds. Begin Cuff instructions.

Cuff

Rows 1 and 2: K1, *P1, K1; rep from * across.

Rows 3 and 4: P1, *k1, p1; rep from * across.

Repeat Row 1.

BO loosely in established pattern. Repeat Sleeve and Cuff instructions for second sleeve.

Finishing

Weave in ends, wash, and block to prescribed measurements.

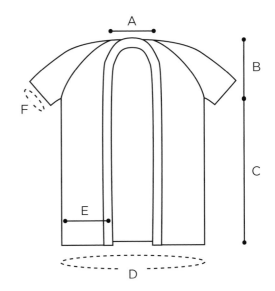

A 5.5 (6, 7, 7.75, 8.5, 9)"
B 8 (10, 11.5, 11.5, 13.75, 13.75)"
C 10.25 (13.5, 13.5, 15, 15, 16.5)"
D 31 (36, 40, 44, 48, 50.25)"
E 6.25 (8.25, 9.5, 9.75, 11.75, 12)"
F 10 (13, 15, 16, 17.5, 18.25)"

Lace Chart A

Row	25	24	23	22	21	20	19	18	17	16	15	14	13	12	11	10	9	8	7	6	5	4	3	2	1
12																									
11				O		λ		/		O						O		λ		/		O			
10																									
9			O			λ		/			O				O			λ		/			O		
8																									
7		O	/	O		λ		/		O	λ	O		O	/	O		λ		/		O	λ	O	
6																									
5			/	O						O		λ	/			O						O		λ	
4																									
3		/			O			O				λ	/			O				O				λ	
2																									
1		/		O	λ	O		O	/	O		λ		/		O	λ	O		O	/	O		λ	

Lace Chart B

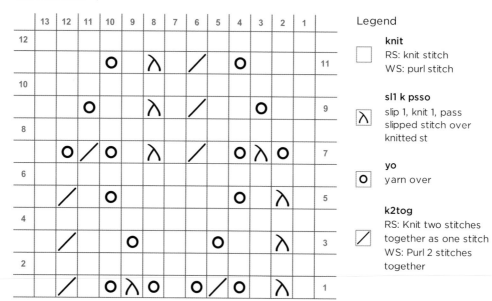

Row	13	12	11	10	9	8	7	6	5	4	3	2	1
12													
11				O		λ		/		O			
10													
9			O			λ		/			O		
8													
7		O	/	O		λ		/		O	λ	O	
6													
5			/	O						O		λ	
4													
3		/			O				O			λ	
2													
1		/		O	λ	O		O	/	O		λ	

Legend

knit
RS: knit stitch
WS: purl stitch

sl1 k psso
λ slip 1, knit 1, pass slipped stitch over knitted st

yo
O yarn over

k2tog
/ RS: Knit two stitches together as one stitch
WS: Purl 2 stitches together

Abbreviations

BO	bind off	M	marker		stitch	TBL	through back loop
cn	cable needle	M1	make one stitch	RH	right hand	TFL	through front loop
CC	contrast color	M1L	make one left-leaning stitch	rnd(s)	round(s)	tog	together
CDD	Centered double dec			RS	right side	W&T	wrap & turn (see specific instructions in pattern)
CO	cast on	M1R	make one right-leaning stitch	Sk	skip		
cont	continue	MC	main color	Sk2p	sl 1, k2tog, pass slipped stitch over k2tog: 2 sts dec	WE	work even
dec	decrease(es)	P	purl			WS	wrong side
DPN(s)	double pointed needle(s)	P2tog	purl 2 sts together	SKP	sl, k, psso: 1 st dec	WYIB	with yarn in back
		PM	place marker	SL	slip	WYIF	with yarn in front
EOR	every other row	PFB	purl into the front and back of stitch	SM	slip marker	YO	yarn over
inc	increase			SSK	sl, sl, k these 2 sts tog		
K	knit	PSSO	pass slipped stitch over	SSP	sl, sl, p these 2 sts tog tbl		
K2tog	knit two sts together						
KFB	knit into the front and back of stitch	PU	pick up	SSSK	sl, sl, sl, k these 3 sts tog		
		P-wise	purlwise				
K-wise	knitwise	rep	repeat	St st	stockinette stitch		
LH	left hand	Rev St st	reverse stockinette	sts	stitch(es)		

Knit Picks yarn is both luxe and affordable—a seeming contradiction trounced! But it's not just about the pretty colors; we also care deeply about fiber quality and fair labor practices, leaving you with a gorgeously reliable product you'll turn to time and time again.

THIS COLLECTION FEATURES

Stroll
Fingering Weight
75% Superwash Merino Wool, 25% Nylon

Comfy
Fingering Weight
75% Pima Cotton, 25% Acrylic

Swish DK
DK Weight
100% Superwash Merino Wool

Shine Sport
Sport Weight
60% Pima Cotton, 40% Modal

Shadow
Lace Weight
100% Merino Wool

CotLin
DK Weight
70% Tanguis Cotton, 30% Linen

Gloss Lace
Lace Weight
70% Merino Wool, 30% Silk

Lindy Chain
Fingering Weight
70% Linen, 30% Pima Cotton

View these beautiful yarns and more at www.KnitPicks.com